THE
UNLIKELY
EVANGELIST

One Man's Journey to Sharing the Gospel Clearly

R. LARRY MOYER
with Kimberly Shumate

The Unlikely Evangelist: One Man's Journey to Sharing the Gospel Clearly
Copyright © 2022 by R. Larry Moyer.

Published by EvanTell, Inc., P.O. Box 703929, Dallas, Texas 75370.

All rights reserved.

Scripture quotations are from The New King James Bible Version, Copyright © 1979, 1980, 1982, Thomas Nelson, Inc., Publishers.

Cover photo: Tiffany Hopwood Photography.
Cover design: Holly Morrison.
Interior design: Shaylana Nelson.

Printed in the United States of America

To the Savior who, by His grace, brought me to Himself, and by His power, freed my tongue to speak on His behalf.

Table of Contents

Preface 3

One
Rooted in Discipline 7

Two
When Drought Comes 19

Three
In the Heat of the Day 31

Four
Within the Sound of My Voice 45

Five
A Season of Firsts 57

Six
A Degree and a Diagnosis 69

Seven
A Foundation of Trust 83

Eight
A New Kind of Wilderness 97

Nine
A Million Reasons to Go 107

Ten
Winds of Change *125*

Eleven
Expeditions in the Western Hemisphere *139*

Twelve
Outreach to the Eastern Hemisphere *155*

Thirteen
Ray of Sunshine *173*

Fourteen
Stories from the Field *191*

Fifteen
The Plane Truth *209*

Sixteen
Big Game, Bigger Reward *227*

Seventeen
The Mission Continues *243*

Conclusion 253

Acknowledgments 257

Appendix
May I Ask You a Question? Tract *259*

The Unlikely Evangelist

One Man's Journey to Sharing the Gospel Clearly

Preface

Speech. The power of communication. It starts with a baby's first gurgle, which soon turns into an utterance of recognition, then finally a conscious expression of opinion. Usually, *I'm hungry!* If not in so many words, then in the shrill of a full-throated and universally understood demand.

The joy of learning new words, forming sentences, declaring statements—it's all part of the growing process that leads every person to a life of independence, relationship, acquisition, accomplishment, and service.

That's if everything goes right.

I wish I could say that everything went right for me. But from an early age, as I went to school and developed as children usually do, I discovered that something was definitely wrong. It came in the form of an inherited speech impediment so severe that I was unable to pronounce "the" without struggling in humiliation. Have you ever counted how many times you say *the* in one day? How would I ever attain my dream of becoming a preacher?

In the insightful words of A. W. Tozer, "It is doubtful whether God can bless a man greatly until he has hurt him deeply." This idea resonates with me—perhaps it does for you as well. It simply means that in order for

God to enable us to do great things, He must first bring us to a point of utter humility. Like Peter as the rooster crowed. Like Paul on his way to Damascus. In this state of helplessness, and possibly hopelessness, we are in perfect alignment for God to move powerfully through us.

In other words, if we interfere with God's work (attempting to help) then we mar the blessing. It is well-known that Moses, the deliverer of the nation of Israel and mouthpiece of God, felt lacking in his speaking ability and was afraid to step into his destiny. But it was in the moment he accepted his own weakness that he began to move mightily in God's strength.

It was because of my own verbal shortfall that I became passionate about speaking clearly. Not just so that others could understand me, but for people to hear the most impactful message of all: the gospel of Jesus Christ. I wanted to speak so clearly that they *could not* misunderstand.

It is my painful past (enduring childhood torment and teen peer pressure) that has shaped me into the man I am today—plenty of humility and, at times, a meekness that can be misinterpreted as weakness. Yes, it's important to stay humble, though the world sees it as weakness. And in the spirit of encouragement, I write this book to share hope with those of you who might be feeling ill-equipped for your journey through this life.

I pray that this offering will prove that as you embrace who God created you to be, despite any physical, emotional, or spiritual challenges, He is faithful to complete what He began. That includes the divine assignments

Preface

specifically designed for you—to declare the message of the gospel throughout the earth.

God brought me to faith on a small dairy farm in Pennsylvania. The call to evangelism took me to Bible college and seminary, which led me to establish EvanTell, a ministry dedicated to communicating God's message of forgiveness and reconciliation. He has sustained me in this ministry for the past fifty years, and shall continue to sustain its work, by His grace, long after I'm gone.

Yes, the cards were stacked against me, and perhaps you're feeling the same way. But take heart, my friend. It's the broken people God uses—the ones that other folks don't believe stand a chance of being used.

Come with me as I share my story of a very unlikely evangelist.

One

Rooted in Discipline

All things were made through Him, and without Him nothing was made that was made.
John 1:3

The roots of a tree run deep, soaking up all it needs from the soil and the environment, inspiring branches to reach ever higher. Nature, one of God's most precious creations, has always given me a sense of peace. It calms the spirit while it ignites the imagination. As a boy, the outdoors was as much a part of me as roots are to a tree, there on our family farm in rural Pennsylvania.

Childhood memories for most of us are rich with nostalgia, carrying with them special recollections that can explain much of our adulthood. We can pinpoint where our current convictions were first fanned into flame, those initial experiences teaching us valuable lessons that shape us into the people we are today.

One of those all-important lessons for me growing up was the discipline of routine. It was something I learned as a small boy, the example set by a very determined father. Dad taught me early on that there were two essentials to creating a productive life—discipline and hard work. Of course, he would say that, being a soul you could set a clock by. No matter the weather, the season, or the seduction of a cozy bed in the frigid temperatures of predawn December, my dad could be counted on as a reliable minute hand of farming mastery.

Mom and Dad were both extremely organized. While my father was in charge of the daily operations, Mom kept the books. But she also had a myriad of skills that every farmer's wife needed if the family business was to succeed. She cooked our meals, canned vegetables, froze meat, and kept the household clean and running smoothly. I never heard either one of my parents say, "I forgot to do this," or "I don't feel like doing that." It simply wasn't in their vocabulary.

Procrastination had no place in our home, either. If the hay crop was ready for bailing, there was no putting it off until tomorrow. The rain might come before then and spoil the nutritional value, and the cattle would suffer for it.

A large part of that stern schedule was the milking of the cows. As a dairy farmer, my dad knew that to produce consistent quantities, our eighteen purebred Holsteins (known for their enormous size and sharply defined black and white spots), were in their stalls ready and waiting at 5:30 every morning, rain or shine.

At 5:00 a.m. on the dot, my father's firm knock on the bedroom door was his less than subtle nudge, as if to say to me and my brother, Johnny, "Alright you two, time to go to work!" This ritual was the same every day, as if there was no other reality on earth—just farm life, predictable tasks, ongoing responsibilities, and more hard work. To us, it was like breathing.

Funny how each cow knew which stall was hers and went to the exact place she was supposed to be—most of the time. Occasionally, a cow would wander into the wrong stall, upsetting its rightful occupant. The confusion in the air and stammering of hoofs was fairly comical, as if it made such a difference where they were fed and milked. Was the morning grain any sweeter in one stall compared to another?

Maybe just knowing where you belonged is enough to stand your ground.

After guiding any wayward animals to their proper space, we would fill the troughs with food, which kept everyone happy, distracted, and in place while the milking machines did their job.

Dad had two machines, one for the cows in the stalls to the left, and one for those on the right. Each apparatus had a large pot with hoses extending from it. At the end of the tubes were suction cups that attached to the cow's teat. When the cow ran dry—no more milk spilling into the pot—it was on to the next. The perfect scenario was to empty each cow completely, so to speak. If a cow was not milked properly it could reduce her production that evening. It took about an hour to milk all eighteen.

Each cow, living up to her full potential, could produce sometimes close to five gallons per milking. When I was little and too small to handle the milking machines, my job was to pour the milk into a bucket and carry it out to the cooler. There, I would carefully transfer the creamy contents into a large container that had two handles. This made it easy to pick up—for us and the truck driver—as we loaded them into the back of his vehicle.

My father's dairy barn

Most of the farm's property was tillable except a twelve-acre patch of woods. The rest of the land was for growing crops, though not for sale. Any dairy farmer can tell you that the wheat, oats, barley, and hay they grow is used exclusively to feed the livestock. Everything that happens on the farm—the labor and all it produces—is for the sole purpose of improving the cows' milking capacity. To a dairy farmer, milk is liquid gold.

With that in mind, one winter was especially cruel with crushing cold and snow that was too deep for the milk truck to make it to our barn. In extreme situations like this, we loaded up the tractor, and Dad slowly drove us with the tenuous cargo, up the icy lane towards the main road. It was about a ten-minute walk on foot, and the tractor wasn't much faster.

I can't remember how it happened (or maybe I don't want to), but somehow one of the milk canisters fell off the tractor as we were skating our way up the lane. We watched helplessly as a milk can of income—a major portion of the day's take—spilled into the snow. The sight was sickening. As a kid, my full understanding of what happened may have been lacking a bit, but I can certainly appreciate it now. It was one of the few times I saw my father upset. Loving my dad as I did, it was a rare and painful sight.

If you like irony, then you'll love this. No one in my family actually drank milk. The entire Moyer clan didn't like the taste, as unpasteurized milk straight from the cow has a much different flavor than the homogenized milk from the carton. We wet our cereal with it—out of necessity—but that was it. My dad used to tease us, saying that we *couldn't* drink the milk because we had to sell it, but he knew the truth. How's that for agricultural hypocrisy?

Cows weren't the only animals on the farm that needed tending. The hogs, chickens, and turkeys all had to be fed, and in the same clockwork fashion—same time, same order, same patient process that kept the wheels of this well-oiled commercial outfit moving. When I felt the hankering to trap muskrats each fall to earn extra money (the pelts worth close to $3 apiece), I would rise at

4:30 a.m. to check my traps, and still make it back by the appointed time.

Being a great lover of the outdoors, I was sure that a farm would be in my adult future with many of the same commitments and responsibilities. But along with that inner feeling of a destiny chiseled in stone was another one deeper still. At the time, I didn't know what it was exactly. All I knew for sure was that waking up to see the sunrise with its golden beams shining brightly through the window told me that there was a God out there somewhere. No, He was *everywhere!*

Nature was always in my bones. I could sit on the hillside and just ponder God's wondrous creation. Being out in the elements—the sun or rain, stillness or bluster, the freshness of the air and all the fragrant things that filled my senses—I could detect a God that had placed this appreciation inside of me for a reason.

Looking back, that time spent outdoors played a significant part in drawing me to the Savior. The most articulate atheist could not have convinced me that there was no God. I knew that He existed and that He was the Creator of all I surveyed.

Spring and summer captivated me with opulent colors and lush foliage, as did the autumn leaves in their vivid shades of red, yellow, and orange. But I confess that fall was my favorite season. Perhaps it was the abrupt change of heart in the leaves of the trees, their usual greenness suddenly striking out in a dazzling display, that wrapped me in awe of what was happening all around me. The sheer scale of it, the miles of spectacular hues stretching out in every direction. This had to be God's backyard!

I felt like I was part of it. It's difficult to explain unless you've experienced it for yourself. Seen it. Felt it. Know that it's so much bigger than you are. That the Artist creating these portraits that morph into brand new works each day, each moment, had placed me within His masterpiece. That is what fall gave me, a feeling of belonging.

My elementary school picture

And as surely as day turns to night, the bare limbs of winter would suddenly appear and reach out as if to grab the steel grey sky. If not for hunting season, December through March brought a certain melancholy to my dulled imagination, as all of God's organic things seemed to wither and die.

So as the seasons in their brilliance and their hibernation circled around, I grew another foot taller and a year older—rooted in discipline.

Where It All Began

"Just two crazy young people in love." Unfortunately, that explanation alone wouldn't be enough to convince their parents to allow my mom and dad to marry.

Although my father, Paul Moyer, was twenty-four, and my mother, Miriam Hershey, was twenty-two, and for reasons I never fully understood, family members would not approve of the marriage. So, they did what any lovesick youngsters would do—they eloped! Running off to Maryland in the waning frost of winter, they tied the knot on February 20, 1937.

For two years, my father worked on the Pennsylvania Railroad, laying track. I can't image how difficult that kind of hard labor must have been, but it paid well. Enough that Dad's built-in discipline enabled him to save the money needed to purchase his first dairy farm. It would be several more years (to the month) before a baby would arrive. All three of their children were born in that same farmhouse in Marietta, Pennsylvania.

My brother, Johnny, came on February 9, 1941. Six years later, my twin sister Lorraine and I shared the birthday of February 19, 1947. And since I beat Lorraine into the world by fifteen minutes, I always teased her about being the "baby of the family."

The day we were born, the snow was deep due to a monster storm notorious for that part of the country. The doctor wasn't able to drive down our lane, so my dad met him at the main road and brought him to the house via his trusty tractor. Clearly, my mother's mettle was forged of strong stuff to deliver not one, but two babies in such dire conditions.

*The earliest picture of my family
(My mother, Lorraine, Johnny, me, and my father)*

The very early memories I made in that initial farmhouse were packed up and brought with us when Dad bought a 127-acre property that stood on the fringe of Elizabethtown. He paid $40,000 for it, and that's where I was raised. Hidden down in a hollow, it was almost as though the farm was too shy to be seen by cars passing by. We nicknamed it Moyer Valley, rightfully proud of the improvements we ultimately made to it.

The aged, weather-worn buildings—the old farmhouse, barn, hog pen, and milk house—all needed a good amount of TLC. My dad and mom eventually transformed this weary homestead into a calendar-picture showplace. Year after year, they upgraded everything, renovating the house, and building an implement shed, tobacco shed, and a garage.

The one-hundred-year-old farmhouse boasted four stories, counting the cellar and attic. It had a spacious kitchen that was easy to love. Upstairs, there were four bedrooms—one for my parents, another for Lorraine, and the third shared by Johnny and me. The fourth room was so tiny it was used mostly for storage. That is until my brother and I grew too big to dismiss privacy issues. At that point, I took the smaller room until Johnny married later and moved out.

When my parents completed the property's restoration, they hired painters to coat every building in pristine red and white. From just a dream in their head to a tangible utopia where they could put down roots for their family, my parents, by the strength of their own hands, made a life for us there.

By that time, I was a teenager. It was a great place to live, to work, and to breathe as my appreciation for nature multiplied. I recall standing there one day, gazing around and remembering what the farm once looked like, and now seeing what it had become. I thought, *This is what hard work will accomplish.* My dad was right. Discipline, in itself, was a reward.

From Top to Bottom

Homes have their own particular personality depending on their age, design, size, and surroundings. But with a house over a century old, our home had more than just character. It wore expressions of a bygone era.

The word "attic" for some people brings images of a dark, creepy tomb full of cobwebs and black widows. The floorboards creak, like speaking with a dusty breath of buried secrets. But our attic was far less sinister, if not ordinary. The attic contained a storehouse right by the chimney where we stowed the hams my dad smoked.

Watching him spread the liquid smoking elixir over the tender meat, I loved how the art of rural survival came in the form of enticing tutorials. There in the attic the hams would hang throughout the winter months. The temperature was so chilly that there was little chance of it spoiling. The only time we ever ate store-bought ham was when the homemade rations ran out.

And just as the attic had its own personality and use, the cellar held a similar utility—butchering. Every year, Dad did his own butchering of several hogs and one steer. January's temperature was an advantage, keeping the beef fresh and easy to cut once it was rendered cold and stiff. Other winter months could be relied upon for slaughtering, as well, but January was trustworthy for its constant deep freeze-like temperature.

The basement of the house was built over a running spring—more like a small canal—which was perfect for washing utensils after butchering. The water ran down a concrete bed to an outlet with a screen over it to keep muskrats and other pint-size creatures from sneaking into the cellar. And with the spring level with the basement floor, one wrong step, and you could accidentally fill your shoes with ice water.

In a separate room, there was a bin to store potatoes and shelves where Mom kept jars of fruits and vegetables she canned. A row of peaches made summer seem as close as the twist of a cap. Everything on the farm felt fresh to me, whether it sat on a basement shelf or it whirled around on a breeze in the rustic outback of my native Pennsylvania countryside.

Life was so very special on the farm. It's the place I loved the most. It filled my days and nights with all of my favorite things. Plants. Animals. Nature on an enormous scale. Beautiful things.

That's why my heart broke the day Dad said that we might have to leave.

Two

When Drought Comes

*The heavens declare the glory of God; And the
firmament shows His handiwork.*
Psalm 19:1

If I went back to that old family property today, I could probably tell you, within feet, where my dad said the worst thing he could have ever said to me: "We might have to sell the farm." I was thirteen or fourteen years old as I stood there, tears welling up in my eyes. In my young life, up until then, there was no day as dark.

Like many people of their generation, my folks weren't exactly transparent. They didn't talk about things openly—their challenges or hardships—but kept them hidden in silence, as if to protect the peace at all costs. They didn't cry either. That kind of emotion was viewed as undignified and self-indulgent. Instead, with poise and composure, they lived one day at a time. Sometimes, in hope of a miracle.

A miracle—I hadn't seen one of those yet, other than the changing of the seasons on the farm that I couldn't fathom leaving. My greatest pleasures and fondest memories were all there. How could we possibly think of moving away? And though Dad mentioned that we might be able to buy another farm later, I wasn't ready to let go of what we had—the only home I had ever known.

At night, I could hear my parents as they lay in bed talking for hours, conversations modulated at a volume for their ears only. The wall that separated our bedrooms muffled any details of financial woes or personal problems. Mom had suffered with severe health issues for several years, and at one point we weren't certain if she would survive. Maybe the money coming in wasn't sufficient for medical care, mortgage payments, and all the essentials that come with running a dairy business.

I struggled to imagine a better house or a finer frontier than the one we were living in now. *Why couldn't we just stay there forever?*

Suddenly, one day, as matter-of-factly as it was brought up, we were told that the farm was paid off. No explanation. No celebratory cake, glass of punch, or balloons. Just, "Oh, by the way, the farm is ours." Nothing more was ever said. But that was their way. You didn't go to therapy sessions, air your dirty laundry, or share painful admissions. Just, *moving on now.*

It is times of trauma that can cause our vision to alter. One or two emotional crashes can leave invisible scars that permanently disfigure our future responses and our way forward. Now, I realize that those tough situations have gifted me with the same resolve my parents had—to take on life with tenacity and courage, one day at a time.

When Drought Comes

The house I grew up in

And just when you think the clouds have all cleared and the sun is here for good, it shines a little too brightly, for a little too long.

I was about sixteen when the drought came. It was so severe that hunting season was postponed in November due to fears that campfires, cigarette smoking, or even gunshots could spark a blaze. The slight rainfall that year meant no crops. No crops, no hay—nothing to feed the cows. The need to buy feed and hay we couldn't grow that summer put a strain on the farm's budget, cutting into its profit.

The natural grasses and landscape turned brown with thirst. The summer months were parched as the wild birds sipped from the livestock troughs and the farm animals hunkered down in the shade of the barn. The fall was a continuance of the same with dry dirt and low humidity.

But heavy worries were doused with the usual steadfastness that my parents always typified. Keep going. No stopping. Everything will turn out with some elbow grease and fortitude. But the bottom line was that good milk production relied heavily on healthy, well-fed cows. And to quickly pivot in business takes savvy and guts. Thank goodness my parents had both.

The lane leading into "Moyer Valley"

As for me, I suddenly realized that with no hay there would be no feed for the cows. What would we do then? My young mind was fearful of the outcome. Dad eventually had to buy hay which was costly and, had it not been for some savings that my parents had nestled away, plus cutting farm expenses in other areas, we would have never made it.

As we weathered the drought that year, I would rate it as one of the most harrowing yet educational experiences of my youth. For someone who regularly works 9-to-5 in a comfortable air-conditioned office, a drought isn't such a concern. But for a worker in agriculture and farm animals—who relies on the highs and lows of a predictable jet stream and sufficient rainfall to make a living—drought is a nightmare that buries itself within your psyche. The mental pressure, emotional anxiety, and physical stress can linger for a lifetime.

Facing this kind of ordeal as a young teen, I never completely recovered. For me, even today, drought is not just a word, it's a feeling—one that reminds me to never take anything for granted. Not even water.

However, by the end of this testing time, the six-month layoff developed in me a sense of dependency on God, and instilled compassion for others who also live day to day on His good grace.

As Better Judgment Prevails

As devastating as a stretch without rain can be, the same can be said for its opposite: thunderstorms. Most common in the late summer and fall months as cooler temperatures in the upper atmosphere clash with warmer air below, deluge is what farmers fear. And we were no exception. We braved flood, hailstorms, sideways wind with pelting rain. All the unavoidable weather events that eventually come with the territory, we endured.

And with the strafing rain that bends delicate wheat shafts, heavy downpours can also destroy corn and barley crops. With adequate force, hail can punch holes into unspoiled tobacco leaves. While it is still salvageable, the tobacco must be sold at a steep discount. These calamities can seriously hurt a farm's income and can even wipe out generations of family toil if the field damage persists year after year.

To an outsider, depending on something as unpredictable as the weather must seem riskier than playing the slots in Las Vegas. That's why being a farmer has to be in your blood. It's a birthright; a seal stamped into your fingerprints that carries over into everything you touch in life. Whether famine or feast, I have learned to depend on God alone.

God will not be directed. He controls the weather, the world, the universe. We had to trust Him, not just for a cooperative climate, but for physical protection. Dad once slipped and fell from about twenty-five feet in the air while hanging tobacco on a rack to dry. My breath caught in my chest as his body hit the ground. Thank God the impact was softened by grace and perhaps an unseen presence sent on a mission of mercy. Whatever it was, Dad simply got up, brushed himself off, and continued working as if nothing had happened. Close calls were always met with that kind of typical Moyer toughness.

Dad wasn't your happy-go-lucky kind of guy. He kept his cards close to his chest—never revealing his emotions—but he was one of the most caring people you would ever meet. He was steady, didn't get angry, and never cursed. He didn't say, "I love you, Larry." Still, I never doubted it.

He was serious and very cautious, always taking into account the dangers of the work and his responsibility to keep him and his family safe. Whether we were working on the farm or hunting out in forest or fields, Dad did all he could to bring everyone home with their eyes, fingers, toes, and everything in between. He was a shield and a sword, a protector and defender. And on one particular day, his hypervigilance and swift reaction would prove its worth.

In my dad's truck was an assortment of tools—a chainsaw, a couple of axes, and a big two-person crosscut saw. But big blades and little boys just aren't a good fit. Johnny was si<u>x</u> years older, and I always envied him when he and Dad went out to the woods on manly expeditions. Now, in my early teens, I was just old enough to start going with them.

Back in those days, people like Dad didn't run to Lowe's or Home Depot to buy building materials. When Dad constructed something, he went out to the patch of woods on our property to cut trees for the lumber he needed.

The project at hand was a new implement shed my father wanted to build. After they had found the perfect tree and marked it, Johnny fired up the chainsaw and began cutting. The noise was piercing as I watched the muscle it took my brother to wield this tool with a temper. I was filled with adrenaline when the tree started to fall.

As Johnny pulled the saw away from the tree trunk, it dragged across his leg and instantly turned the blade bright red and his pants crimson. As blood gushed from Johnny's leg, the meager handkerchiefs and towels we used to try to stem the bleeding weren't nearly enough. Getting him back into the truck, Dad raced for home.

I guess you could say that the apple doesn't fall far from the Moyer tree, because Johnny somehow believed that his condition wasn't dire enough to call for an ambulance. He sat on the porch, growing pale and weak, and I waited for my big brother to pass out. Yet he stayed conscious as he was rushed into town to the doctor's office.

This lesson was not lost on me: while there is a time for conspicuous bravery, there is also a time for surrendering to those who still have a healthy amount of plasma in them to make rational decisions.

Thank God the chainsaw didn't hit the femur bone, and the doctor was able to stitch him up and send him home. This was a day that I marveled at—the accident could have been so much worse.

Reverence and Religion

Is there a difference between revering God and believing in the gospel of grace? Being raised in a God-fearing home that had no knowledge of what Christianity was really about—the deeper meaning of what Christ did and why—I can tell you that there is a very big difference.

I wouldn't say my folks were legalistic but they embraced some pretty strict ideas. We blessed our meals with repetitive legalism: "God is great, God is good. Thank You, Lord, for this food." We attended a denominational church every Sunday, but the sermon lacked any real sustenance found in the Word of God. Instead, the focus was on rules—lots of rules.

On one occasion, my mom found me trimming my fingernails on a Sunday, which was considered an Old Testament no-no as it would be considered "work." With a gentle yet firm admonishment, her point was made. Not with anger. My mom never showed her temper. But it was her fear of God—to avoid upsetting Him or doing something that could be mistaken as rebellious—that she faithfully held to.

It was because of my parents' occasional rebukes that I learned God was someone to be obeyed. Their stern warnings didn't make me think any less of God or see Him in a negative light. It actually solidified the importance of revering Him.

Mom and Dad loyally practiced what they preached. No farm work was done on Sundays, other than milking the cows—that was absolutely necessary. But that was it. It didn't matter if the rain was coming the following day and the hay needed to be baled for fear of it spoiling, Dad never baled hay on Sunday.

Instead, my parents made the day fun. On some occasions, they would take us into town to the icehouse where a generous size block would be crushed before taking it home to make ice cream. Other times we would go on picnics. But whatever we did, it centered around their promise to set aside Sunday for God and family.

I loved growing up on the farm

In hindsight, I'm convinced that my folks' God-fearing mentality instilled in me what would later bring me directly to Christ. Because of the living example of their devotion to God, they established my respect and need to align myself with Him. It was important that above work, above personal needs, there was God—*nothing* was above Him.

Though my dear parents were more concerned about not doing anything wrong to offend God, I feared that they were missing the truth: the nature of people is inherently imperfect and broken. Jesus' sacrifice on the cross covers that sinful nature. I hadn't reached that understanding yet, having just started to read the Bible as I approached my teens. But I can see now how God used every small chance to mold and shape me for the service that lay ahead.

From the time I was a child gazing around at the splendor of the fields, rivers, and sky that enveloped me, I always asked the same questions: *Where is this God? Where does He live? Where can I find Him, meet with Him, talk to Him, feel Him, know Him?* I wondered all these things while never doubting He existed, just afraid He might frown on me if/when I did something wrong. As a kid, I wasn't even sure what those wrongs really were or how many I was liable to commit.

I knew God was there, and I understood that He was big, powerful, and in control. I wasn't afraid of Him—usually. I simply respected Him. Still, I couldn't escape a nagging feeling that I wasn't doing enough to please Him. It was through my grade school years when I noticed this profound awareness of God.

Maybe raindrops are the perfect illustration of what faith looks like when the first glint of God trickles down into a childlike mind. There is a drip, then a little more, until we're able to absorb the full heart of His feelings about us. Then there are droughts in life that keep His Word from reaching the dusty soil of our spirit. I suppose it's a normal cycle while we're here fighting against earth's elements and our own flesh and blood emotions. Some emotions more overwhelming than others.

Like when Johnny ran out the door with his gun in anger to seek revenge.

Three

In the Heat of the Day

*Let your gentleness be known to
all men; the Lord is at hand.*
Philippians 4:5

Rage. Sometimes I think there must be an "angry" gene that skips over one person and multiplies in another. What is it that makes certain men and women prone to fits of anger, striking out so quickly to attack while their better judgment seems helpless to step in? My brother Johnny struggled with it. So did I. Once, my temper flared, and my mom said to me, "You better watch that temper. That's what makes people murder." That instilled a fear in me that one day I might do something horrible.

It's a reminder that within every human being—no matter how passive they might seem—lives a combination of good and bad, patience and impulse, kindness and cruelty. God created us to be completely perfect, compassionate, and gentle. Then the fall happened and suddenly, our light radically shifted, and we would be tested in ways we were never designed to be tried. Love may live outwardly most of the time but anger can sometimes consume us, stealing away our gentler side.

How different we must be now than how we started out.

On the farm, we had a beautiful calico cat named Tippy. I can still see her lying there like a rag doll with a bullet in her head. Her thick furry coat of gold, black, and white stained with blood; her tail and limbs hanging limp. My mother went upstairs to cry in private as Dad followed her. We were sad and shaken by the evil thing someone had done—destroyed a family pet on the border of our field as she was probably searching for mice.

Johnny suddenly grabbed his rifle and tore out of the house as Mom begged him not to go, but with no avail. There was a real chance someone was going to get hurt that day, not that I could blame him. There was a loving animal that never hurt a soul lying dead, brutally killed for no apparent reason.

Now, you might be thinking that I'm a huge hypocrite for hunting wild game—also God's creatures—while showing a special pity for an animal that curled up on my lap and kept me company as I did my homework. But there is a hierarchy in nature, from the top of the food chain to the bottom.

However, man takes it a step further, where necessity to survive is replaced with the desire for revenge. And so, the clock sluggishly ticked by as we waited for the outcome of Johnny's retaliation.

Rules of Engagement

Dad taught us how to handle guns, and safety was always at the forefront of his mind. I don't think he could have forgiven himself if something were to happen to Johnny or me. He showed us the right way to carry a rifle or shotgun—pointed straight up or straight down, not swinging carelessly back and forth. He explained the importance of getting ahead of your hunting dog before firing, and never shooting into the brush without knowing what it is you're shooting at.

I knew a farmer who didn't take that precaution during a rabbit hunt. When his beloved dog ran into the bush after the game, the leaves stirred as the animal fled. The farmer pulled the trigger and struck and killed his retriever. Yes, I understood the power of a gun.

Johnny was a much better shot, but he was older, and his eagle eye and spatial awareness inspired me to be as good as him some day.

We hunted a variety of smaller game such as groundhog, rabbit, squirrel, and pheasant. During hunting season, which lasted from early November to just after Thanksgiving, we were allowed a specific number of each game per day—four rabbits, six squirrels, and two pheasants (male Ring-necked). Big game, such as elk or deer, required a license and had a limit—one buck per season, unless you had a doe permit as well.

There was one exception to these hard and fast rules and that was for groundhog. This destructive varmint was such a menace to farmers—digging holes, damaging property and the equipment that fell victim to their burrows—folks were legally allowed to shoot as many as they wanted, all year long. They were unprotected, though a license was needed if you went off your own property to hunt them.

During one summer, I circled our entire 127-acre farm twice each evening and killed a total of thirty-three groundhogs! Dad's pride was evident, though he didn't say as much. But then, he didn't have to. He had other ways of showing his affection.

Teaching Lorraine how to shoot

My father's hunting skills were often coupled with his generosity. As bushes rustled with small game, Dad knew exactly which side of the brush the rabbit would exit and would position me on that side to take the shot. When a squirrel scurried up into tree limbs, Dad would motion me to the perfect place where that squirrel soon would become visible. These inconspicuous gifts were his way of showing that he cared—quietly but continuously.

By a living example, my dad taught me how to put others first, to silently give without fanfare or publicity. In sharing moments that spoke louder than words, I heard him say, oh, so clearly—*I love you, son. I may not say it out loud, but I do.*

Farming is about as tough a job as any you'll find, especially dairy farming. And to reward my brother and me for our hard work, Dad would let us hunt all season long—with the exception of Sunday, of course. Even if, by law, we could have hunted on Sundays, my father was committed to putting that holy day aside. God mattered more than any squirrel, rabbit, or deer.

But on any other day, we pulled on our brown hunting duds and set out. The gear we wore had a pouch for the rifle shells and another one for the game you shot. There were no fluorescent orange safety vests, yet. Besides that, we had all we needed.

For small game, I carried a 16-gauge double-barrel shotgun. For large game, it was a rifle, but not until I was old enough. Like most kids growing up in the country, my first gun was a BB gun that Dad gave me around age nine. Then, I graduated to a shotgun when I was twelve. I will never forget the morning Dad stopped me as we prepared to go squirrel hunting.

"Larry, I think it's time you carried your own gun," he said, as he placed a single shot .410 in my hands. It was a milestone. In my father's eyes, I was a man.

Every Saturday during small game season, I would go out just after sunrise into the land that I loved so much. Through the yard to the fence, then across the meadow I would walk as autumn and its colors encircled me. Amid the bright sunshine, blue sky, brisk breeze, or when November's more typical days prevailed, even the clouds, grey overcast, and damp earth clinging to my feet couldn't cast a negative shadow over hunting day. I was where I belonged.

Some Saturdays Dad and Johnny would come with me, but most of the time I was on my own. I loved being out just after it rained—the sound of my soggy boots muffled by the water-soaked leaves. It gave me the opportunity to reflect on the One who created it all. In a way, I was hunting for God—that elusive Person I couldn't seem to track down. But it was the times by myself that grafted my dad's brand of silent yet ever-present love deep within me.

Dad also allowed me to go out every weekday after school, as well. To make this possible, he would stay and do the farm work. It was an act of kindness that gave me a clear understanding of how much my father cared. Though a man of few sentimental words and even fewer hugs, he loved me in a way that I couldn't miss. He gave me the gift of trust. Of freedom. Of joy. And there in the countryside, I would stay until night approached.

Then just before sunset, I would come back home . . . to find the cows already milked.

More Than Skin Deep

Twins have a connection that is hard to describe. They share the same womb from conception and begin life together. They are a collection of two on a joint venture in close partnership. When I took my first breath of air, there was someone who quickly followed and experienced the exact same thing. There was a person walking around with much of my own DNA, almost like another part of me.

My twin sister Lorraine and I shared similar brown hair and eyes, but our behavior was dictated by old-fashioned gender stereotypes. I had the spirit of an explorer while Lorraine was shy and introverted. Her thin build and quiet demeanor suggested that she was a pushover, but that certainly wasn't the case.

Living out in the country meant that neither of us had many friends—none that came over to play. But we found company in each other as we romped in the sandbox underneath the front porch. Trucks, balls, and other toys kept us occupied. Then, one day, Mom made the mistake of trusting us with paint and brushes. The benches in the front yard needed a good coating, but Lorraine and I decided that the paint had another purpose just as useful. Flinging a brush-load of pigment in my sister's direction, it was a direct hit.

A battle ensued with shrieks of laughter and ended with two children wearing more paint than pride, and a dog that got caught in the middle. The benches did get finished, but Mom wasn't exactly amused by our methods. I still smile thinking about my sister and me and the many joys we shared made sweeter because we were twins.

My sister and I attended first and second grade in a one-room schoolhouse that stood at the top of the lane. It was only a ten-minute walk if you took your time. And since Lorraine lagged behind my energetic stride, I moved at a gentler pace to stay beside her.

Biking with my twin

Our teacher, Mrs. Ammons, was strict, and gave us so much reading homework that my folks eventually wrote a letter telling her to lighten up. And being in one room with different age groups, we became adept at ignoring her lessons directed at other students. Topics were split into days of the week—history one day, science the next, math the day after that.

From third through sixth grade, we attended Rheems Elementary School, which required us to ride the bus. But wherever I was, Lorraine was nearby, and vice versa. We couldn't have been closer and spent the majority of our time together until we were about ten years old. That's when I grew strong enough to lift a fifty-pound bag of feed and work the farm with Dad. Lorraine stayed inside to help run the household with Mom.

This separation allowed me to get better acquainted with my brother Johnny as well as spend treasured time outdoors with my dad—working, hunting, and learning important lessons from him.

For instance, after a hunt, Dad and I would take the game into the kitchen where it was skinned. I loved those moments with him, talking about the hunt and the day's activities. Our connection was one of respect and cooperation. Our love for each other, beyond words.

King, the family dog, felt much the same way. Wherever we were, he was there wagging his tail.

King of the Farm

When thinking about dogs, many of us imagine them as a common part of the family. Big, tiny, medium sized, lap dog or working dog, they all have a special place in our heart and home. But not every dog has a lap to snuggle in or a hearth to sleep next to. Farm dogs can have a very different place and purpose, and Dad's sole reason for buying our beagles, Nellie and Becky, was for hunting.

Beagles are best known for their high energy and intensity for hunting rabbits, although they will chase after a jackal or wild pig if given the chance. They can be used individually or in packs, which drives their competitiveness to its zenith. They're also hound dogs which makes them prone to roam. But at fourteen inches high and an average weight of twenty pounds, a beagle is perfectly compact to get into brush and ravines, yet stout enough to intimidate small game.

We kept Nellie and Becky in a separate pen by the barn with a doghouse for when it rained. In the nippy winter months, they slept in a pen in the barn. Keeping them at arm's length didn't seem to affect their cheerful disposition. They were with us year-round, but it was when hunting season began that they were put to use.

Nellie and Becky were friendly and loved affection, but Dad didn't let us play with them, as it could affect their natural laser focus while out in the field on a hunt. And as for guarding the house, their excessive barking might be good for scaring off critters, their social disposition would do little in confronting a midnight burglar. That job was better left to the professionals.

A preferred breed for K-9 officers in police work, German shepherds make great guard dogs—loyal to their owners and assertive to unwelcome strangers. Known for their smarts, strength, and protective streak, their growl and menacing canine teeth could convince anyone to turn and run.

Our German shepherds named King and Queen (brother and sister) came home to us as pups from a breeder. This duo would be the objects of our love, as we could pet and play with them as much as we liked.

I always wondered if Nellie and Becky felt any animosity about the way they were treated (barnyard and doghouse) compared to the freedom that King and Queen enjoyed. But the straying nature of beagles cannot be compared to the steady staying power of shepherds.

Queen was a bit of a loner and favored her own space. King, on the other hand, craved company day and night. He simply needed to be close to us. Whether we were pulling up fence out on the property, hoeing a crop of tobacco in the field, or pulling weeds one row at a time, King was there right alongside us. Almost human-like, some dogs can be our friend, and live to please us. They find their purpose in making humans feel loved. King was that friend.

Me with our dog, King

But it was no secret that King favored Dad. Maybe he could sense how dependable and steadfast my father was, giving King the sense of safety and acceptance. After all, they spoke the same language—silent appreciation. I could hardly blame King as long as I was his second choice.

When Johnny Came Marching Home

With so many animals in and around our lives, you wouldn't think that the loss of one little cat could send the wrath of Johnny running out the door with a gun in his hand to make hell pay. But Tippy was such a sweetie. Beautiful calico coloring, conversational meows at mealtime, and her sandpaper tongue that tickled when she licked you, Tippy was instantly missed and deeply mourned.

Johnny had been gone an hour now, searching for the person who killed our precious family pet. I think we were terrified that the police would call with the news of an arrest, that maybe Johnny's infamous temper had finally taken things too far. Overwhelmed with fear, we waited anxiously for Johnny to come home.

"Big John" as some called my brother was a volunteer fireman and loved the comradery with his cohorts. They shared the same work ethic, the same fearless fortitude. When the siren suddenly blared in the distance, he would look at my father with that, *'please, let me go'* look. And seeing the determination in his eyes, Dad almost always said yes.

Johnny worked hard at everything he put his mind and muscle to. He also believed that everybody else should have the same attitude. It bothered him when people took time off to goof around. Case in point: there was a public swimming pool near our farm, and on hot days when the pool was open, the sounds of young people shouting and splashing drifted our way. It irritated Johnny so much—kids having fun while he baked in the sun hoeing tobacco—that he couldn't keep his aggravation to himself.

"They don't know what hard work is!" he would often grouse.

Johnny loved driving big machinery and taught me how to drive a tractor. The day he let me take the wheel alone was one more pivotal moment that changed the way I looked at myself. Having a brother so much older, Johnny and I didn't connect in a lot of ways. But I longed to gain Johnny's approval—for him to see me as an equal.

When I got old enough, Johnny started taking me squirrel hunting with him, showing me all the best places to find them. Then a friend of Johnny's invited him to a neighboring county to hunt rabbits. My brother was eager to go and could have easily left me behind.

"Why don't we take Larry with us?" he said to his buddy.

My big brother wanted me to go with him! Another milestone. When we got there, about two hours away, it was like a fortune hunter's dream albeit on a much smaller scale. But through the eyes of a young teen, it was heaven. Everything I shot at, I hit. The best part was that I made Johnny proud.

Now, Johnny was gone, out chasing down a man who killed our cat. There was a restlessness in him, and perhaps my brother was chasing more than he knew.

In the years that followed, he couldn't control his weight and his foot pain got worse. Slowly, his love for hunting faded. As time went on, and my love affair with all things outdoors continued to grow, tension between the two of us grew as well.

He finally came home the day Tippy was killed, without satisfaction. He never did catch the guy.

It was better that he didn't.

Four

Within the Sound of My Voice

*Preach the word! Be ready in season and
out of season. Convince, rebuke, exhort,
with all longsuffering and teaching.*
2 Timothy 4:2

"Dad, where are you?!" I yelled into the lonely mountain terrain. "Answer me!" Each step I took seemed to take me further away from where I started—from the safety and security of my father's ever-watchful eye.

Amongst the northern red oak, American sycamore and beech, the eastern white pines, hemlock and sugar maples, the gullies and crevasses that separated the crests and pikes, there was always the possibility for hunters to lose their way in the rugged outback of Pennsylvania—a risk I had been warned about. Now, suddenly, I had met the same fate in that majestic wilderness. At sixteen years old, the learning curve for hunting was still ongoing, and that fact was never more apparent than on the day I found myself lost, alone, and vulnerable.

Dad always dreamed of getting a buck but that wish had yet to come true. Then his dream became my dream. Passion doesn't begin to describe the obsession we both shared for bagging a buck, and my father thought maybe, if I got a doe permit, it would bring me one step closer to that goal. I applied for the permit, received it, and the morning of doe season, the two of us headed for the mountains.

My 9th grade school picture

With the excitement of Lewis and Clark on their daunting expedition, we trekked into the woods. After walking for a while, we sat down quietly in hopes that other hunters might spook a deer our way. But waiting was much harder than hiking and sitting there was difficult for me to do.

"I'm heading to the top of the ridge to see what's around," I told my dad as he stayed behind.

I strode through the mountainside for a glimpse of the surrounding landscape. Hopefully, I could shoot my first doe. What a prize that would be to bring home wrapped in my father's approval. But as I trod up the embankment and through the lush canopy of tangled tree limbs, I suddenly realized I hadn't been paying attention. Somehow, the worst had happened. *Where was I?* More importantly, *where was my dad?*

Getting lost in the Pennsylvania highlands when the temperature drops below freezing wasn't something I ever wanted to experience firsthand. But in my brave yet careless enthusiasm, I had taken off for an adventure without looking where I was going—or rather, where I had been. Now, I was confused and completely turned around, not knowing where I was.

My screams caught in the thick brush as I cried, "Dad!" but I heard nothing back. He couldn't hear me. I kept screaming as I wandered, feeling guilty about all the deer I might be driving out of Perry County. But I was so afraid, I didn't dare stop.

A Way of Escape

On a perfect day when all was well, hunting in the gorgeous outdoors with Dad, I still wasn't completely happy. The satisfaction—the fulfillment I was searching for, expecting to find—wasn't there. Looking back, I wonder how I stayed the course with God. It's only natural to lose hope, to give up on an invisible Someone who never answers you. *Where are you, God?* I would think. I just couldn't seem to find Him.

For such a young person, my attention for the finer details—each crisp blade of grass, the delicate veins that run through a single leaf, the dazzling sparkle that raindrops flash in the sunlight as they pool on the ground, the rich amber designs in the bark of a tree—everything in nature shouted the glory of God.

I remember hearing once that "nature is God's greatest evangelist." That image is the essence of my deep love for His creation. Yet, God Himself kept escaping me. It didn't seem fair. I cared so much. I was sure He was the ultimate Artist that crafted the earth and the treasures found in it. Why wouldn't He show Himself to me personally?

In our house, the Bible wasn't studied as a family, yet it was revered as the Word of God. And as so many Christian homes lack the practice of daily reading, I thought perhaps if I began to expose myself to that holy book, God just might reveal Himself to me there. Taking its leather binding in my hands, I allowed the pages to fall open on its own.

Sometimes the scriptures made sense. Sometimes they didn't. But more times than not, the Bible would part to the book of John, and there, it would unlock mysteries. Within those verses of truth, I discovered the good news.

Did I know what the words meant, or that their meaning would change gradually? No. But God did. He was beginning a work on the inside of me, planting seeds in an open heart and mind. As I read more and more passages, studying the scriptures, His light grew brighter and my comprehension of God's love for me settled deep inside.

It was during this time that I went to a tent meeting where an animated evangelist shouted theatrically about "superhighways to hell" and warned everyone to stay on guard. The preacher was sensational to watch and listen to, but he failed to explain how to get to heaven. Only where to find the road that led in the opposite direction—to my frustration.

Soon after that, a friend of my father came over to the house and told him that he had gotten "saved!" He was now a Christian—a believer in Christ. As a mere bystander listening to him carry on about what changed in him, how he was touched, and his future was now filled with optimism and promise, I felt even more curious, and slightly envious. Still, he offered no explanation of how it happened or what it really meant.

If only our family talked to each other openly, I could have asked my dad. Instead, I was left to wonder, but I knew I was getting closer to what I was searching for. Perhaps it was something I needed to tell God directly. Not ask, like "Where are you?" but to declare, "I believe in You," whether I could see Him or not.

It was nighttime. The farm was quiet. I knelt beside my bed and closed my eyes. "God, the best I know how, I am coming to You. I believe Christ is my only way to heaven." In my young mind, there was nothing scarier than the thought of not making it to heaven. And a recent and terrifying dream of hell and Satan, no doubt, shaped that statement in no uncertain terms.

The Unlikely Evangelist

The next day, as I sat in biology class, I noticed a calm and peacefulness had entered my soul. All the unhappiness and unrest were gone. The void was filled. The storm on the inside was gone. I felt secure. Something supernatural had happened the night before as I knelt next to my bed. God had entered my life!

Yes, something had happened, though I couldn't say precisely what it was. I just knew that it did. I had come full circle. From seeing God's fingerprints throughout His creation of nature to Christ being present with me. I had traveled from creation, to Creator, to Christ. And in that strange sweetness, the vision of my divine purpose appeared. I could see it, and it was a revelation.

I was put on this earth to be an evangelist. Like Billy Graham and many others like him.

This inner knowledge of what I was made for gave me a sense of exhilaration and anticipation for the future. I suddenly realized what my dad's friend was talking about. What it meant to be saved from the emptiness and isolation that comes with being human, separated from Jesus. He was a part of God, and God was in everything. Now, He was in me.

With my new salvation came a different opinion of our liberal church, the same church we had always attended. The pastor was known around town for telling dirty jokes and entertaining inappropriate topics. His Sunday morning messages repeated, "God loves you, now go love others," but they were just words. And as I sat there one Sunday morning, I almost leapt up from the pew to correct him, to tell him there was so much more to God's plan and purpose than what he was telling us. Then I wondered if he even knew.

But most of all, the fear of death that used to haunt me was lifted. I had lost a classmate to a car accident, and on another occasion, a friend's father had died. Because of it, I couldn't stop worrying about my own demise, envisioning me or a family member lying in a coffin. The thought consumed and frightened me. I was fixated on death—or I used to be. Now, the fear was completely gone. I realized that God was with me, all the time, no matter what.

He would protect and guide me from here on out.

The Laughter of Children

In every child's life there are decisive moments that help shape them, for better or for worse. And it's difficult to imagine something more damaging than a child not fitting into their community of peers. I vividly recall such a moment and its lasting effects.

A teacher called on me to come up and read in front of my third-grade class. Unbeknownst to me, I wasn't able to. My mouth opened and the words came out—or tried. But I stammered as the room fell mortally silent. My fellow students were frozen in delight as I struggled to push out the sentence. My anxiety reached a trembling pitch when the teacher took pity and said I could sit down. My classmates could tell there was something off about the way I spoke, and they giggled and whispered with poorly hidden grins.

That's when I knew that I didn't—I couldn't—talk like everyone else.

It seemed weird to me now that my mom, dad, and siblings never mentioned this obvious discrepancy. But who cares how articulate you are on a farm, milking cows or baling hay? Now, the kids at school were laughing at me. Teasing me. Making fun of the way I couldn't even pronounce the word *the*.

I never told my parents about the abuse at school, which only made the problem worse. There were no school counselors as there are today. No social skills taught to kids. No special "helps" for those with inherited defects. Certainly no parental backup for moral support. I didn't even say anything to Lorraine. I was all on my own, almost. God was there.

After the humiliating exposure of my speech impediment, I stuck to sports, which required little verbal communication. And with my defined arm muscles from heavy farm labor, I excelled in baseball, hitting more than my share of home runs. As time went by, there was one kid at school I thought I could trust. But this needed testing.

Outside the lunchroom was a table set up for kids to play games before morning classes. This particular classmate seemed nice, and maybe a little kinder than the rest. He was playing a board game that interested me, so I meandered over and asked him a question about it. But instead of answering me or inviting me to play, he laughed at me, loud enough that other kids joined in.

They mocked and harassed me, more than I could stand. I counted the minutes until the day was over when I could run home to safety—cows never laugh at you.

As if things weren't bad enough, there was one more heartbreak on its way.

Doctors Know Everything

It was a common cold—that's all it was. Stuffy nose, scratchy throat, a cough, a bit of a wheeze. But you never can tell when it comes to childhood sickness. And being a dutiful mother, Mom took me to the doctor for a professional opinion. We were ushered into the examination room where I stood alongside the doctor as he sat in his chair.

"Well, young man," the doctor said, as he gently pressed a stethoscope to my chest, "what do you want to do when you grow up?"

I wasn't completely sure if the good doctor would understand hearing a little kid say, *I'm going to be an evangelist*, so I opted for a simpler answer: "I'm going to be a speaker."

His eyebrows raised as he continued to listen to my lungs. "Well, you can give that up. You could never do that with your problem."

What did he say? I was suddenly reeling. He sounded so sure of himself, said it so matter-a-fact, that I had no other option but to believe him. The news was crushing—the thought of not being able to do what I knew God wanted me to do. What was I going to do now? What could possibly be better than to tell people about the gospel? Without knowing it, this one man had utterly devastated me.

As my mother and I walked out of that office, a shadow of dread covered me. The doctor's esteemed diagnosis was soaking in, and I believed I might never be able to accomplish the things I truly felt I was called to do. Outside, the same world turned; traffic, pedestrians, sun and sky all still there as before. It was only a rotten cold that ailed me, and I just needed fluids and rest. Yet, in that moment of absolute defeat, I thought, *If a truck comes along and hits me, it would be a relief. What's the use of living if I can't speak out for God?*

Days, months, years passed, and I could feel my emotional strength giving out to an inner voice, a constant antagonist, telling me, *You're an outcast. A freak of nature. Stupid. You can't even do something a child can do—talk!* The torment continued into high school with more peer pressure and cruel jokes at my expense. One afternoon, it all became too much. With my head in my hands to hide my tears, I prayed, "God, if you will help me with this speech defect, I'll always use my voice for You."

As if waiting in the wings for me to pray those very words, God did exactly that. A divine power entered me, just as it had years before as I knelt by my bed. A strange and wondrous control was given to me over my speech. The impediment was still there, but God was providing me the ability to make my tongue speak like it never had before. And with that empowerment, I was renewed with spiritual fire and hope.

I was well on my way to fulfilling my destiny.

My senior year

And just as my father eventually heard me screaming out to him on the mountainside that terrifying day of doe hunting and answered, "I am over here!" God also answered me in my blackest moment. In both instances, I was finding my voice and moving in the direction that would lead me back to where I ultimately belonged.

Dad and I never talked about how I panicked on the mountain, and I was too embarrassed to bring it up. He was only a few hundred yards away, yet it felt like miles of impassable separation. I'm sure my dad was asking himself why I was so afraid when he was so close.

Eyes rely on light to see and are easily deceived in the dark. What some people view as weakness, God uses as strength. He gives favor to the helpless. He brings direction out of confusion. He enables us to love with a broken heart and provides a way out of the desert.

My heavenly Father was never far away—He was always within the sound of my voice.

Five

A Season of Firsts

How much better to get wisdom than gold! And to get understanding is to be chosen rather than silver.
Proverbs 16:16

A concrete jungle—a place where the city skyline of high rises, bridges and infrastructure had replaced the trees, hills, and mountains of my beloved home on my family's farm. Where the animals had been traded for cars coughing fumes in thick traffic. Where the fresh smell of earth beneath my feet and the dream of getting my first buck gave way to cement sidewalks and streets filled with people. *What have I done?*

Months before, as a senior in high school, I was too naive to know that there were such places as Bible colleges. So, I asked God to raise up one for me to attend. Shortly after that, my friend David who had been a student at Philadelphia College of Bible, told me of his experiences there. He recommended PCB as it was highly focused on the Word of God.

But first, I needed to see the college for myself. My parents were not opposed to it, but their fear of the inner city kept them from taking me. Then David mentioned that he and some others were driving to the campus, that there was a "college for a day" program, and that I should come along to see if the place and curriculum was something that appealed to me.

"There's room in our car for one more," he offered. It was as if God had answered two prayers at the same time—a college to pursue my destiny, and a ride there. I started the following fall term in 1965. This began my four years of study at PCB.

Leaving home for the first time was a big deal, especially since no one in my family had gone off to college before. All I could think of was, *have I made a mistake?* Everything was so different in a metropolitan area. I was quickly overwhelmed—just a small farm boy in a big wide world I knew little about. My eyes had been opened, and I was worried. Feeling adrift in a sea of other students, I was on my own again. I didn't even know what to bring; Mom had to tell me what basics to buy, like deodorant.

Turns out, the first student I met quit and left for home a week later due to stress. That was unsettling. The college campus was downtown, nestled into the mayhem not far from the Liberty Bell. Venturing off site was unnerving since I had no prior contact with diverse cultures or disparaging social differences. There were no fields, no meadows, no barn with cows and the usual chores that were such an integral part of my days.

I missed Lorraine and Johnny. I missed the comforting voice of my mother, and the reliable presence of my father. I missed our dog, King, and getting to wake up in my own bed. I missed the schedule and rhythm of my old life. Everything was all jumbled up in a brand new and not-so-shiny package that was downtown Philly. *Was it too late to change my mind?* It would take some time to know for sure.

School of Hard Knocks

When classes began, all of the fuzzy feelings I had about my calling to evangelism came into sharp focus. I knew I was where I was meant to be.

My college buddies and me
(I'm the third one from the left)

I lived in the dorm with a roommate that first year. But everything that I loved on the farm drew me back to visit home every weekend. Hopping aboard the train on Friday night for the hour and a half-long commute was a saving grace that helped me through the early acclimation period. The house I grew up in was as warm as always—perhaps even more—filled with familiar sounds, smells, and memories that reminded me of how fortunate I was to belong there.

But studying the Word was my joy, even wrapped in grueling academia. I immersed myself in learning, to the point where I was placed on academic probation—studying so relentlessly, my performance actually began to suffer. I guess you could say it was the fear of failing. Who knew that a student could work himself into fatigue and confusion resulting in poor grades?

It was during my second year that I found my stride—within the student body and in my social life. Initiating an outdoors club, I started to relax, and even date. However, I had made a commitment not to get serious about a girl, much less entertain the thought of marriage, until after I graduated. These were unwritten rules not easily ignored as I found out from watching my fellow singles, especially the female ones.

If you went out with a girl once, you were technically dating. If you went out a second time, you were preparing for marriage. At least that's what everyone seemed to think and something I took very seriously—to avoid. Instead of intimate gatherings, my friends and I would go to a park nearby and find a patch of sun to unwind.

A Season of Firsts

We didn't go to movies, but we did enjoy an occasional evening college event.

It was during this time at Philadelphia that I was given some very sad news from home. Somehow, amidst all of the years of growing up, stretching my wings and finding my path, our devoted German shepherd had gotten older too. I couldn't help but think that King would have been near my father when he died.

King was my father's shadow—a loyal friend. King's sister, Queen, always wanted to be left alone. And as loners often do, she left this world with a whisper. But the precocious charisma of King (and now his absence) nearly pushed me to tears as Dad and I quietly memorialized him during my next visit. King was buried beneath a tree near the house, and it was in these tender moments that my dad showed his gentler side. It only served to remind me that nothing lasts forever. People, nature, beautiful animals, like seasons, they change as the years roll by.

On a happier note, with my third year of devoted study and peer networking, I was elected president to the second largest organization on campus, the SMF (Student Missionary Fellowship). This put me in charge of the annual missions conference, a huge five-day event held on campus. It was a blessing as God orchestrated my one-on-one rapport with British evangelist, Major Ian Thomas, whose words still resonate with me today.

"All that Christ is is available to the one who is available to all that Christ is."

Major Thomas recognized my passion for ministry and did everything he could to encourage me to follow that dream. How incredibly fortunate I am to have met and known such great men of faith. They were there—as if by divine appointment—to inspire and guide me to establish a future ministry that would last longer than I would. Hindsight tells extraordinary testimonies of God's sovereignty. I give Him all the glory for what has transpired in my life. His path is not always straight, but it will get us home.

At the end of my third year, I ran for the biggest office on campus held by a student and won by a respectable majority. I would return after the summer break for my final year as student body president. Of course, my parents were happy for me, though going to college wasn't something they could identify with. Just as long as their son was doing well, that was enough for them.

All of these meaningful experiences strangely triggered a conflict within me. My studies were about devoting myself to God, and less about doing what I wanted, which was going after a buck. I was beginning to think that discipleship meant "all pain and no fun." Was I still allowed to enjoy hunting anymore? I wasn't sure.

Instead of going home after my third year, I took an interim pastor position for the summer. Mom and Dad agreed, even though it would leave the farm shorthanded. The pastorate was at West Liberty Baptist Church right outside DuBois, Pennsylvania. I stayed with an elderly woman named Mary DeLarme who opened up her house for me, rent-free with meals provided. She was a godly woman who had lost her husband and two of her sons. She taught me so much about being a Christian through the consistency of her contentment and her sunny disposition. During that time, I also held down a construction job.

My second car, a Camaro

If there was any question I might have about my performance during that summer, it was answered when the leadership of WLBC wrote a letter to the president of Philadelphia College of Bible, singing my praises. While humility is something I am often commended for, I must humbly say how this profoundly impacted me. They said I was a great preacher!

God was smiling on me. I could feel it. And it was during that final year at PCB, one week after Thanksgiving on a visit to the farm, when God smiled again with one more incredible gift.

There were six of us—my brother Johnny, Earl (my best hunting buddy), myself, and three others. Out in the countryside I loved so dearly, we gathered at a deer camp my parents owned. That particular morning, we each headed in separate directions.

Finding a nice ridge to survey my surroundings, I paused by a tree. All of a sudden, I heard a sound behind me. There, I spotted him—a magnificent buck. The moment was electric. I squared my stance and settled my feet into the moist ground. As I narrowed my sights for a clean shot, adrenaline coursed through me. All of the hard work—the growing, learning, tracking, waiting—was about to finally pay off. I held my breath to control the nerves and squeezed the trigger. And ... he dropped.

It had finally happened. My very first buck!

My fellow hunters helped me tie him to the trunk of the car, and we headed home. Dad was delighted, and Johnny was sincerely happy for me. I still remember Mom getting on the phone, "Larry got his buck!" she gushed to a friend. All of my dreams were coming true, all in God's perfect time.

Reaching the End—Almost

Conflict can be a double-edged sword. An inner conflict can pierce a hole in our hearts as easily as an exterior opponent can with a pointed opinion or a calloused comment. And as I diligently studied scripture to gain knowledge of the Bible, I began to think that hunting might be a selfish act.

Were believers allowed to enjoy themselves this much? I wasn't sure that being a devoted disciple of Christ allowed for much fun. To surrender hunting to God—choosing one favorite thing over another—was a choice I fought to reconcile for some time. Finally, I made my feelings known to God in a prayer one night: "Even if I can never pick up another gun again, You have my life. I surrender it to You. I'm Yours completely." The struggle was over.

Governing the student body along with my scholastic schedule and personal time kept me busy my final year of school. As a perfectionist, I poured myself into everything I did. What a journey it had been, from a tiny one-room schoolhouse to a pulsing Philadelphia campus filled with books, teachers, professors, and companions on the same trajectory as me. Even with my speech impediment, I had reached a level of success that made my childhood trauma a distant memory.

Still, there was something nagging me—something a professor said—that continued to gnaw away at my self-confidence. She told me that I was "lazy" when I spoke. "That's your problem, Larry. You're just not trying."

So, I worked harder and ... *it only got worse.* It seemed that I was still misunderstood and not living up to some people's expectations. After all of the effort I had put in, it was frustrating and slightly discouraging to hear such a thing.

In 1969 I finished college in Philadelphia with my undergraduate's degree—a Bachelor of Science in Bible. The accomplishment instilled a renewed sense of purpose, that I was on my way to becoming an evangelist. Though I hadn't planned on going to seminary after college, through much prayerful consideration, I decided that having a master's degree would only increase my knowledge of the Bible and open more doors.

Dallas Theological Seminary impressed me the most. But it was in Texas! That meant I could no longer go home as readily, or go hunting. The very thought of being separated from my beloved family, farm and animals, woods, hillsides (not to mention the wild game that beckoned) was a heavy choice. It was one that didn't come easily, but it came just the same. Dallas Seminary it would be.

The summer before my first year in Dallas, I got a second pastorate as an interim pastor at Trinity Baptist in Catonsville, just outside of Baltimore, Maryland. This was an excellent opportunity to learn firsthand a pastor's responsibilities and helped prepare me for my future ministry in evangelism.

Soon, word got out about a new young speaker, and Christians from neighboring communities began to come to hear me preach. It was a powerful time of worship and teaching. At the end of the summer, as a going away present, the church leaders gave me a book with dollar bills tucked inside of it—each bill getting bigger as I turned the pages.

Blessing upon blessing. Needs met. A path laid out before me. God's goodness was so evident and present that my fears were overcome before ever taking root. It's an amazing thing to feel the Holy Spirit's wind at your back, to accelerate in the direction you know you're being called. But there was still a matter of my speech that seemed forgotten by God.

A Season of Firsts

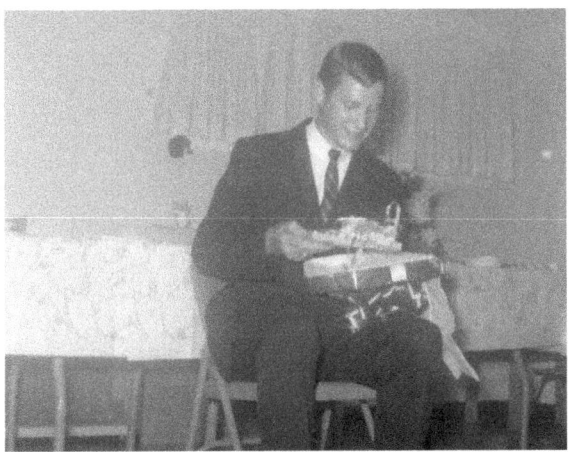

The book of dollar bills

Moses struggled in his speaking, but he had Aaron by his side. The apostles were rugged fishermen with flaws and failings, yet even they were sent out two-by-two. I had to believe that God would supply a partner for this unlikely evangelist as well.

With my bags packed, I quit my part-time job as a gas station attendant and moved out of the parsonage. Dallas Seminary was calling to me, and a four-year graduate degree was on the horizon.

Six
A Degree and a Diagnosis

> *[God] has saved us and called us with a holy calling, not according to our works, but according to His own purpose and grace which was given to us in Christ Jesus before time began.*
> 2 Timothy 1:9

Another enormous city awaited. But this time, I was prepared. It was 1969 when I arrived at Dallas Theological Seminary for a four-year graduate degree—Master of Theology. Still, Texas was a world away from my home in the resplendent natural setting of Elizabethtown, Pennsylvania. Traveling across several states would be another milestone that came with its share of sacrifices.

The landscape was flat and paled in comparison to the majestic woods and mountains of Pennsylvania. There were no grand and elevated landmarks that stood high above valleys of lush greenery. And the extra distance would keep me from going home whenever the mood struck—only on Thanksgiving and Christmas would my family see me. No more hunting small game on the weekends, basking in the forest air or the savory smells of my mother's cooking.

My sister Lorraine found a job as a secretary for an insurance company in Elizabethtown, and my brother Johnny still worked the farm with Dad. To my relief, home was one place that never seemed to change, at least not drastically. It was a plot of earth made of more than a fenced boundary line and a field of crops. It was cozy and comforting with its late summer sun, cool fall evenings, and a hearth in winter that kindled the closeness of the people and place I loved the most.

But the anticipation of achieving a lifelong dream was enough to forfeit the solace of the familiar for the anxiety of the unknown. It was God's love letter to mankind—the Bible and Christ's redemption story—that pulled me to new horizons. And just like God's wonders of nature, He provides a season for all things to come to fruition. The Lord's grace went ahead of me, watering the soil as I came to Dallas, finding unexpected support waiting there.

His name was Dr. Haddon Robinson, a preaching professor with the gift of communication unlike anyone I had ever witnessed. Somehow, I knew when I met him that he would make an indelible mark in my Christian journey. Every word he spoke had meaning. Every thought, every idea came out in a way that made perfect sense. His unique delivery and clarity sparked an even greater desire in me to do the same. He was someone to emulate and admire.

A Degree and a Diagnosis

It was a marvel to watch him capture the imagination of his students, challenging us to strive for more: to learn more, practice more, be more than we were when we walked into the room. Everything he said found a place within me and stayed. The spiritual food he offered wasn't milk but meat, yet easy to digest. His concepts filled me. His speaking drew me to his classes again and again. Every discourse, workshop, and address he gave left me spellbound, intently listening and learning, finding fresh perspective of God's gospel to the world.

That entire year set the precedence for the next three years as I decided what to major in. The advice I was given was to choose something that afforded the most access to my favorite professor. That was an effortless decision. I chose Bible Exposition as my major, which came with my two preferred teachers—Haddon Robinson and Dwight Pentecost.

As I sat in a lecture hall one day, soaking in the heavenly insight of Dr. Robinson, he said, "The ones I help the most are the ones who come after me," meaning, those students who actively pursued his classes and him personally would benefit all the more. I thought, *Look out, Dr. Robinson, here I come!*

The following year, I immersed myself in his inventory of divine understanding. I'm sure he couldn't help but notice the same enthralled apprentice hanging on every syllable with an endless supply of zeal. Each term, there I was, bright-eyed, enthusiastic, tapping into his reservoir of godly knowledge. With my constant presence, coupled with a steady stream of questions, I was a sponge to his holy water, drawing up all the droplets of sparkling wisdom and discernment found in his inspirational current. Simply put, he was a river of motivation.

My passion was palpable to everyone as I preached in front of the class for the first time. Recognizing what God had placed inside of me, Dr. Robinson said, "Clearly, you've already had a lot of experience." This was due to the parsonage positions in Pennsylvania and Maryland, which was now evident through my comfort level and intensity. And having been an evangelist before a professor at Dallas Seminary, he was aware of what I was capable of from the start.

He said to me, "Larry, learning how to preach is learning how to think. If you think clearly, you will preach clearly." I took that advice to heart, where they remain etched. Those words also became an ongoing prayer, that God would continue to hone my talents and fuel my fortitude for service.

Imperfectly Perfect

As strange as it may sound today, no female students were allowed at Dallas Seminary when I attended. It seems antiquated now, but in the 1960's Bible belt, it was normal, if not always appreciated. This made the apostle Paul's suggestion to the Corinthian church personal: "It is good for a man not to touch a woman. Nevertheless, because of sexual immorality, let each man have his own wife." *There was the answer. But where would I meet a girl on an estrogen-free campus?*

Paul goes on to write, "For I wish that all men were even as I myself. But each one has his own gift from God.

A Degree and a Diagnosis

But I say to the unmarried ... It is good for them if they remain even as I am" (1 Corinthians 7:7-8).

Unfortunately, like many young men who have not been given the "gift of celibacy," I counted myself within those ranks. Thus, I was often reminded by the Holy Spirit of what Jesus said, recorded in Matthew 6:33, "But seek first the kingdom of God and His righteousness, and all these things shall be added to you." Words to live by, and I did.

During my second year at Dallas, the inevitable happened—I met a young woman. The circumstance was not at all extraordinary in an era where it was common for a person to find their significant other through a blind date. However, the setup was unusual even by the standards of 1970. It was a *triple* blind date!

It's always a friend that starts the wheels-a-turning. This particular friend, Chris, had gotten a date for his sister, but she had two more friends. Truth be told, I really wasn't excited about the prospect of a blind date, *but he was persistent!*

"I tell you what, I'll give you first pick of the three girls." I guess men haven't changed so awfully much in decades since.

He told me that the girl named Tammy was tall and also a gifted vocalist. "She's the cream of the crop," he admitted referring to all three women—including his own sister. Of course, he shared that secret in the strictest of confidence. With thoughts of my future grounded in evangelism, *it wouldn't hurt to have a spouse with the talent to sing.*

It was evening in early fall when we all got together for the State Fair of Texas located at the sprawling Dallas fairgrounds. As first impressions go, I appreciated that Tammy was a Christian, but she was still figuring out spiritual issues—how to grow closer to the Lord, and if her own salvation was assured. Chris was right, she was tall. And lovely. And fun to be around. Though I would later discover that her opinion of me wasn't quite as positive.

Nice guy, she thought, *but if I never see him again, that's just fine.*

Our first date: Tammy and I are in the back

I wouldn't have called her icy but thank goodness the second date began to thaw her perception of the "on fire" seminary student with the speech problem. We drove to Turner Falls State Park in Oklahoma, a popular touristy playground in southern Oklahoma close to the Texas border. It was comfortable being with her, and I soon realized that my speech deficit didn't deter her from wanting to spend more time with me. Early in our relationship, I believed she was someone I could get serious about.

That intuition proved true when, two years later, we got engaged.

No Man Is an Island

Just as I had made peace with the idea of not going home to Pennsylvania during the weekends, there was an ironic twist during the summer of 1971 and again in 1972. Now, I would spend much of two summer breaks out of the country. The trips were headed by a missionary pastor who had an extensive network throughout the West Indies. This evangelistic tour took us to seven islands, which included Antigua, Nevis, Montserrat, St. Martin, Dominica, and the U.S. Virgin Islands of St. Croix and St. Thomas.

We went by small plane. The only correspondence I had with Tammy was by letter—I could write to her, but she was unable to write to me due to my frequent island hopping. But God used that separation to reveal just how much I loved and missed her.

I stayed with the local pastor except for my time in Nevis, where I was put up at a guest home left to the church by a woman who had died in a ship disaster. She specified in her will that the house was to be used for visiting missionaries, a generous gift.

I thought I understood what poverty was until I was faced with the grim reality of what villagers lived with day in and day out. It was a shock to the system discovering that the reason I wasn't staying with the pastor on the island of Nevis was because he could scarcely afford to feed his own family, much less a young healthy American man.

When he did serve a meal to me, he would then go out fishing at night to find food for the rest of his family. On one island, we all ate from a mound of rice served atop a small table—the four of us residing on small tree stumps surrounding the table. We shooed the hungry chickens away as they pecked at our food. After that awakening, I never took anything for granted again. Witnessing that level of lack is hard to shake, and should be.

Most churches didn't have a musical instrument—no piano, organ, or a worship team that we commonly find in American churches. But the sound of those village parishioners lifting their voices to God in praise filled any physical, financial or material deficiency they were struggling with. Nothing but a heavenly blend of modesty and gratitude that could outshine any keyboards and guitar chords found in the plush sanctuaries back home.

There were instances when the electricity would go out during a service, but no one reacted because it happened so frequently. They just kept singing, praying, speaking the Word of God that shed its own light on the hearts and minds pressed together within those fragile walls. There could be 50 in the congregation or upwards of 200 depending on the size of the town. These numbers would swell the second summer I went. But it didn't really matter. The unity and selfless cooperation made it a place of undeniable fellowship.

The West Indies was a place of tropical blue waters kissing silky beaches, sprinkled with salt of the earth—where no one was an island.

Just to Be Clear

My time at Dallas Seminary was sprinting by. But a worst-case scenario loomed—I might need a part-time job to survive while my full-time evangelism gained traction. Becoming established enough to work solely for God could take some doing. Connections were an important part of laying the foundation for my forthcoming ministry and career.

In order to get the word out, I wrote everyone I knew a "Declaration of Availability" letter to share my intentions. That I was going to be an evangelist and was available for speaking engagements during summer months and after graduation. This meant delivering sermons any place, any time, to any crowd.

As far as I was concerned, anywhere was at least *somewhere*. If asked, I would have shown up at a backyard barbecue if I thought people would listen. And that actually happened (after all, I was in Texas), where a pastor invited me to speak at his barbecue, then preach at his church, then at a weeklong outreach.

Slowly, I began to build contacts. By the time I completed school, my calendar would be nearly full. Dr. Robinson was impressed by my determination and wrote his own letter to the entire alumni of Dallas Seminary encouraging them to invite me to speak at their respective churches. This single endorsement would result in nearly twenty immediate requests, and more would follow in the years to come due to that letter.

But I had one more year of school to get through.

It was during graduation year that students elected the top four preachers within their class. What a privilege it was for me in 1973 to be chosen as one of them. This selection of standouts would have the honor of speaking during Senior Preaching Week at chapel—one per day, Tuesday through Friday—just prior to graduation. It was a thrill to be cast in such a distinguished light.

This was followed by a trip to Memphis, Tennessee, where I spoke at an evangelistic outreach. The experience was anointed. After finishing my sermon, two people approached me—a Christian and his non-believing guest. The man who had yet to trust Christ said something to his friend that has remained with me as a benchmark.

"It's the strangest thing," he admitted to his Christian friend, confused but convinced. "He struggles when he speaks, but he's the clearest preacher I've ever heard."

It was an awesome statement as the believer later relayed it to me. The man found the message within the sound of my voice, just as it was—unapologetically flawed—but perfect for God's purpose. Hearing his reaction to it lifted me up and grew my courage to continue on the unlikely path I was following.

How often we forget that our Creator makes us exactly who we are, for work He designed in advance for us to do. An individual lacking some skills will still succeed and even surpass expectation if God ordains it. "For it is God who works in you both to will and to do for His good pleasure" (Philippians 2:13).

A Degree and a Diagnosis

After listening to me preach my fourth-year sermon from 2 Timothy 2:3-7, Dr. Robinson shared what I considered to be a revelation. "You have such a gift, Larry. I just wish you knew how to make your mouth pronounce the words right."

"What did you just say?" I asked him, bewildered but intrigued.

"You just need a speech therapist," he answered.

My mentor, Haddon Robinson

I could scarcely believe that I was in my mid-twenties and had never been told that before. And per Dr. Robinson's referral, I soon entered the office of speech pathologist, Beverlee Warren. Her demeanor was kind yet thorough as she tested me for possible conditions. At the same time, I had the opportunity to tell her just how important the visit was to me.

Understanding that I came from Dallas Seminary with considerable public speaking experience, she looked amazed. "How did you get here?" she asked.

At first, I thought she meant which road did I take to find her office. "What do you mean?" I said, hoping not to sound sarcastic.

"You don't get to where you are without help," she added.

This left the door wide open for my testimony. I took my time, painting a realistic portrait of my childhood on the farm, public school trauma, college with its own brand of challenges, and now achieving a master's at a renowned seminary. And as my descriptions mingled with my usual broken vernacular, I could tell she realized that something very special was happening.

When I finished, she said, "God has obviously done something. Now, I'll take you the rest of the way." She went on, "You were born with something called an articulation disorder—where the tongue has no idea where to go to make certain sounds."

The diagnosis was an epic disclosure. It made sense that my parents never saw the significance of my speech impediment since dairy farming doesn't rely on fancy orations. You got paid for working, not talking.

After that initial consultation, Beverlee saw me once a week for a year at the cost of $5 a visit. She gave me words to practice, and drilled me each time I came in. By the end of that year, she was satisfied with the outcome. This didn't mean that I spoke perfectly, and I have a feeling that was God's idea.

A Degree and a Diagnosis

"You're there, Larry. Though you may never reach a point where people hear you speak without a slight speech defect, don't let it bother you."

Dr. Robinson responded much the same. "Larry, it will only help you. People identify with the underdog. That's what you are."

And I still agree with him. I believe my speech was (and is) a necessary element to a powerful testimony God gave to me. I articulate messages as best I can. That is God's will. I've been advocated for by people who invested their time and energy, helping to lay the groundwork for a ministry that had yet to bloom. That's faith: the assurance of things unseen. That's what they gave to me.

Graduation day came in early summer of 1973. Shoulder to shoulder, our black caps and gowns lent the 80 students in our class a unified dignity as the rolling applause of over 1,000 guests filled the sanctuary of Gaston Avenue Baptist Church. Flash bulbs erupted like popcorn on a hot stove as cameras snapped loved ones receiving their coveted diplomas, signifying four long years of study, work, and accomplishment.

Pockets of proud family members and friends cheered as each name was called out. My parents and siblings couldn't make the ceremony. Apart from their fear of flying—they had never been on a plane before—a dairy farm isn't an automated business. There are animals to feed, cows to milk, chores that cannot be left undone. I wished they could have been there, but they were with me in a way that's hard to explain. Their love was a part of me, wherever I went, and in everything I did.

I could barely feel my feet beneath me as I strode across the platform in the blur of a packed audience. Among the faces, I found Dr. Robinson, Dr. Pentecost, and other professors who had devoted valuable years to my education. As I took the diploma and stepped from the platform, I was greeted by a man of great reputation—a man known worldwide—Dr. Charles Ryrie. The authority and approval in his voice eclipsed the excitement of the moment—if that were possible.

"I know God is really going to use you," he said to me.

Was he there that day I spoke in chapel? Did Dr. Robinson plant a seed of support in his ear during a conversation? I didn't know. All I could do was smile and receive what he said with profound thanks and gratitude. It was the biggest thing that happened that day—beyond earning a degree, seeing the expressions of joy on the faces of Tammy and her folks, embarking on a fledgling ministry. Dr. Ryrie's validation was evidence of what was to come.

But first ... I had a girl to marry!

Seven

A Foundation of Trust

But we have this treasure in earthen vessels, that the excellence of the power may be of God and not of us.
2 Corinthians 4:7

There is something about seeing your bride for the first time all dressed in white, a vision of elegance and beauty, that sends a man's heart soaring. It was 8:00 p.m. on Saturday, May 26, 1973, when Tammy made her way down the aisle toward me.

Since that initial blind date three years before, meeting a statuesque young woman with the lovely singing voice, I would eventually realize that I was courting my future wife, though this revelation didn't happen overnight. Tammy was attractive, smart, sweet, and I enjoyed her company from the beginning. Her interest in me at first was purely spiritual, but our mutual affection for each other blossomed in the months that followed.

Before meeting me, Tammy hoped that she would marry a farmer as she loved the outdoors—a love we shared—just as she couldn't imagine herself marrying a pastor. As it turned out, she ended up with both.

Two weeks after graduating from Dallas Theological Seminary, I married the love of my life.

The ceremony was held at Trinity Baptist Church in San Antonio, Texas, at Tammy's home church in the town she grew up in. The service was emotional and joyous, lasting nearly an hour with 300 guests in attendance. It was a wedding with all the usual romance and fun that such happy occasions bring. Clasping her father's arm, Tammy walked slowly down the aisle as her mother's eyes glistened.

My fiancée was an ethereal angel in a pale dress with a petite train that flowed from her hem in the back. A veil sprinkled with delicate lace flowers and tiny white pearls framed her pretty face amid the soft sanctuary light. She cradled a bouquet of fresh yellow roses, white spider lilies and white carnations arranged with baby's breath. I inhaled deeply trying to control the pounding in my chest.

It's difficult for men to put into words the splendor of lace dresses, pastel flowers, and sentimental tears without threatening their own masculinity. I guess we just swallow the lump in our throats and try our best not to show how touched we are by them. These mental photographs have never faded, nor do I expect them to. They remain, unyielding to the tarnish of time.

The matron of honor was Tammy's sister-in-law Ann Cameron, and five additional friends made up the bridesmaid party. My best friend from Dallas Seminary, John Vincent, stood next to me as the best man, along with five groomsmen that included Tammy's brother and cousin. All the men wore crisp white tuxedo jackets paired with pressed black pants. Looking around at my friends and soon-to-be family members, I so wished that my own blood relatives could have been there.

A mirror of graduation day, Mom and Dad were kept from the wedding due to farm responsibilities and time constraints. Yes, they were physically absent, but very present in the spirit as I carried them with me to that altar. Johnny and Lorraine couldn't make it either. However, two old friends from Pennsylvania did travel to Texas to take their place, sitting in the front row where Mom and Dad would have sat.

Dr. John Reed, a preaching professor from Dallas Seminary, who also counseled Tammy and me the entire year prior, came to San Antonio to marry us. The melodious piano and viola performance by Tammy's friends—also music majors from North Texas State University—added to the gentle evening ambiance. And still another dear friend of hers from church sang a tender solo accompanied by the pianist.

So many familiar faces, loving words of promise, and a kiss to seal our holy pact, made those moments as perfect as you hope they would be. Tammy was mine, and I was hers. We suddenly belonged to each other through a sacred vow of trust, tied together beyond any untying. I had found my other half. As I gazed at her through a veil of euphoria, my wife smiled back at me.

The reception was held in the church fellowship hall with music, dancing, laughter, cake, and a wealth of well wishes. Late that evening, Tammy and I left for Comfort,

Texas, spending our first night together as man and wife at His Hill Ranch—a camp retreat that Tammy had been to several times as a teenager with her church youth group. It was a place that stowed fond memories for her as she received spiritual encouragement there that would later carry her faith into this season of marriage and ministry.

We tied the knot on May 26, 1973

The following day, we returned to the home of Tammy's parents in San Antonio to open the generous wedding gifts we had received. Tomorrow, Tammy would begin her final week of teaching music class at an elementary school in Irving, Texas, to finish out the year before retiring. It was a door closing in order for another to open. We would both be free to start afresh.

So, we said our farewells on that blessed Sunday and headed back to Dallas, filled with anticipation for all that lay ahead.

Our honeymoon came the week after that.

The state of Colorado is recognized for its craggy mountain ranges, clear lakes and rivers, forests of velvety firs, and picturesque vistas you find on postcards. We arrived in Bayfield late afternoon to enjoy a proper honeymoon at a rustic little hideaway called the Safari Lodge. This resort was a quaint cluster of small cabins conveniently nestled close to the natural sites, fishing holes, and hiking trails.

Though I was proud to have graduated seminary completely debt-free, for a young couple just starting out, we had to be frugal. Our cabin, the gasoline for the drive, and our food expenses cost a total of $150. How's that for thrifty!

For one glorious week, we backpacked the rugged hills, took in the gorgeous scenery, and relaxed by chilly mountain waters catching brook trout. The rest of the time, we did . . . *what honeymooners do.*

A House Built on a Rock

For years, I had carried a burden to create a grace-driven (not guilt-driven) evangelistic organization. My vision for it was straightforward: a ministry centered on the clear presentation of the gospel and simple explanation of biblical text that was easy to understand. After childhood discouragement followed by hard study and strenuous therapy to tame my wayward tongue, that vision was finally turning into reality.

Our first home in Garland, Texas

To start with, Tammy and I rented a tiny efficiency for the summer while our tract home in Garland, Texas, was being built. The apartment was owned by Dallas Seminary, which made it affordable. Thank goodness for Tammy's savings account that bankrolled our new abode. Tract homes were common at that time and also convenient. We simply perused through various floorplans, chose a particular design that fit our needs and finances, and waited the three months it took for the builders to complete it.

It was during this time that I founded Encounter International. At the encouragement of Dr. Robinson, the association was incorporated as a nonprofit on April 5, 1973. This would provide room for the ministry to grow and aid in its financial demands. Dr. Robinson understood my vision—a ministry that would not only serve the United States but the entire world. We had an attorney draw up a charter and bylaws.

Our budget for that first year was $11,000. This lean season of seed planting would require all of the imagination and creative resources I could muster. And like any small living thing with proper care and provision, the fledgling nonprofit grew. Soon, I needed a secretary assistant, a position that was filled by Janice Miller, a friend of Tammy's. She faithfully served for several years before starting a family.

Mike Cocoris, also a graduate of Dallas Seminary and already in full-time evangelism, joined the association in 1974 to further its expansion and status. Together, we worked persistently for the next five years until Mike accepted the pastorate at Church of the Open Door in Los Angeles, California. Though I was sorry to see him go, I was blessed to have him in those early years.

Yet, with numerous other ministries espousing the name "Encounter" in its title, I felt it muddied the waters and confused people as to which ministry we were. It made sense to find another name—one that reflected the true image I had for this unique organization. Its new name would be grounded in the Greek word for "gospel" which is "evangel."

Two years later, on September 17, 1975, the association's name would officially change to EvanTell, Inc.—which represents "Evangelists telling the gospel."

I had launched a platform in which to address the two greatest needs I saw in current evangelism: the first was to present the gospel in the clearest way possible. Other evangelists I had heard never seemed to explain in plain terms why a person needs Christ, and also why Christ's death and resurrection were the only basis for a right standing with God. The second need was for something called "expository" preaching—that is, to thoroughly study the Bible, and carefully explain scripture in a way that people can absorb and relate to.

EvanTell's mission was to present the gospel to the masses without complicating it. And in order to establish a firm foundation for this very important endeavor, God chose five godly men to comprise the initial Board of Directors: Dr. Haddon Robinson, Dr. Harold Hoehner, Mr. George Cramer, Mr. John Maisel, and myself.

All we needed was a workplace. That would come through George Cramer, who owned an office complex at the southeast corner of LBJ and Midway in Dallas. He charitably donated our initial office space in that building. We kept it for a year before moving to another location still in Dallas.

Thanks to Haddon Robinson's contacts and endorsement letter, my visibility reached into the surrounding communities and beyond. In an era when social media was decades away, advertising came in the form of radio, hardcopy, and word of mouth. But even under such archaic circumstances by today's standards, my calendar was quickly booked every other week, keeping me busy with weeklong outreaches at local churches.

It was becoming common knowledge that God had gifted me as an evangelist, and soon my speaking schedule stretched three years in advance with invitations coming from all over the country. EvanTell's boundaries were ever widening. And as the ripples of a pebble tossed into a pond steadily magnify in size and scope, our territory pushed outward beyond Texas.

EvanTell's first office space donated by George Cramer

I praise the Lord for all of God's help—human and divine. We were blazing a trail based on an ideology that never wavered: present the gospel clearly through understandable language founded on careful, prayerful study of scripture.

The work was hard, but fruitful. The fields were ripe. The harvesters were few. And that in itself was a troubling thought.

The Bible tells us that all believers are called to share the gospel. Still, I was noticing that most Christians rarely shared the good news, not because they didn't want to. It was simply because they were afraid that they lacked the words and/or the ability to explain it properly. In my deepest heart, I couldn't ignore that necessity.

People needed to be equipped to present the gospel if the body of Christ was to multiply and thrive.

Bad News / Good News

Clichés... we hear them so often, they become embedded in our vernacular and society. This makes them perfect for teaching and memorizing. From that realization, I created a method of instruction that leans on one of the oldest clichés around: "I've got some bad news and some good news."

This Bad News/Good News analogy was the ideal training tool for people anxious about their attempts to share the gospel effectively. The bad news is obvious—we are sinners who deserve eternal separation from God. That's why the good news—receiving the truth, trusting in Christ, and bringing that message to others—is called the Great Commission.

In 1979, I was invited by Dr. John Reed—head of the Homiletics department at Dallas Theological Seminary and the pastor who married Tammy and me—to become an adjunct professor of Evangelism. That clearly accelerated my ministry as I started teaching that same year until 2017 when the course was discontinued. I continue teaching there to this present day, but in the Doctor of Ministry department.

Also in 1979, when I had just finished speaking at a weeklong outreach in Pennsylvania, the church pastor said something to me that resonated in my bones.

"Larry, our people would love it if you would explain to them how to share the gospel."

There it was, a confirmation of the void I suspected was haunting the church. I agreed and taught the Bad News/Good News method to his congregation before returning to Dallas. Later, this same pastor told me, "I don't know why you're not teaching this to more people. We have folks going out and sharing Christ for the first time in their lives. And there are new converts sitting in front of me every Sunday."

Upon his words, I made it my mission to teach this outline, which continued to make an indelible impression on all those who heard it. Believers were getting the tools they needed, and were now confident that they, too, could remember and master the technique.

Making it as simple as a familiar cliché, I wrote down the Bad News/Good News method. It would eventually be compiled in a booklet titled, *May I Ask You a Question?*, the first cover designed by a brother in Christ named Fred Randall. That publication is still available on EvanTell's website today at www.evantell.org. It then developed into a mini seminar, and the video titled, *You Can Tell It!* would release in 1984.

These first years of ministry were rich with experiences that filled my days with the energy to press forward. I visited various states such as Iowa, Texas, Utah, Illinois, Minnesota, and Pennsylvania in my pursuit of spreading the gospel. Tammy came with me and sang prior to me speaking. Most of the time we traveled by car and came home to the Dallas office exhausted but fulfilled. Life was good. But there was one thing missing—one small but precious thing.

A Sacrifice of Love

There he was, three days old, wrapped in a cotton blanket, vulnerable, beautiful. He opened his eyes, and as Tammy and I gazed at him, we instantly knew he was our baby. Tammy reached for him and cradled him with all the affection any biological mother could have.

Months before, a teen mom-to-be was in an impossible position: keep her baby and struggle beyond her capabilities, abort the pregnancy, or give the child up for adoption. Thankfully, she chose the latter, and even prayed that the infant would find a safe and loving home with a godly family.

The baby was born in 1982 in the town of Independence, Missouri. The young mother (we'll call her Lexie) considered going through an adoption agency. However, when she learned from her physician that he knew of a Christian couple in ministry wanting a child, she was thrilled at the news, and gave the doctor permission to handle the arrangements.

Pastor Don Hawkins, whom I had known since 1969 as a fellow student at Dallas Seminary, offered his house in Kansas City as a "transfer" place. Since private adoption in the state of Missouri wasn't practiced, Lexie and her parents brought the child across the state line into Kansas. Lexie's attorney met them at the Hawkins' house with the proper paperwork.

It must have been excruciating to sign a document saying she was letting go a part of herself. But we hoped that she understood that her little boy would be loved and cared for as much as any child could. She held her baby for the last time before she and her parents left. Tammy and I arrived after that.

The grace of God was all around. The attorney was a member of Don's church and agreed to act as lawyer for free. He smiled, "I'm not going to charge you for the adoption work. You see, I was adopted—into the family of God—and I wasn't charged a thing. So, I can't charge you."

Tammy and I flew home later that day with our newborn son, David, in a spirit of faith that Lexie wouldn't change her mind during the next six-month waiting period. For now, we were technically only David's guardians. This gave Lexie ample time to reconsider and take him away from us. But we hung on to hope. When six months had passed, we finalized the adoption through a Dallas attorney.

David was officially ours.

Our first family photo

In the last few years, by God's grace, I was able to forge a marriage, a ministry, and now a family. I could see God building in my life, brick by brick, on a foundation of trust—trust in Christ, in His purpose, in His power. But the journey had just begun and would soon take me across an ocean.

Eight

A New Kind of Wilderness

*And He said to them, "Go into all the world
and preach the gospel to every creature."*
Mark 16:15

Amsterdam—just the name can create images of old-world charm and modern-day debauchery. It's a complicated place of historic heritage, cobblestone streets, and strands of pictorial canals that meander through the town.

This capital city of the Netherlands was my introduction to Europe in 1986. Though I had traveled to the West Indies in 1972; to Ontario in 1975; then New Brunswick and Manitoba, Canada; this was my first time visiting "the old country."

Amsterdam was a vibrant metropolis, brimming with a centuries-old past, rich in antiquities, and a multinational population. After World War II, Amsterdam experienced an influx of races and religions. There are over 150 different cultures that call Amsterdam home—one of the widest varieties of nationalities of any city on earth. What better place for Billy Graham to hold a conference for evangelists from across the globe.

Thanks to Dr. Robinson's letter to the organizers of Amsterdam '86, I was being considered to attend. The vetting process for those requesting admission was thorough and specific. A few months before the conference, I received a notice of acceptance. I would leave that July.

Billy's vision was to bring together 8,000 evangelists from 180 countries—a total of 10,000 people that included 2,000 observers, staff, volunteers, and press. The Amsterdam '83 conference drew 4,000 attendees. This time, according to the United Nations, between 10,000 and 20,000 people would be turned away. They said it was the largest event of its kind ever held in Europe.[1]

I flew into Schiphol Airport near Amsterdam, then traveled to my hotel located near the conference center and checked in. In my late 30's now, it was exhilarating to experience a worldwide network of fellow evangelists.

According to an article in Decision magazine, "Never before have so many men and women exercising the biblical gift of evangelism gathered in one place at one time to exchange ideas, to learn, to stretch spiritually in order to fulfill more purposely the ... work of an evangelist."[2]

God had placed me there *for such a time as this*.

Commonly referred to as the "Venice of the North" due to its many attractive waterways, Amsterdam

---

[1] https://www.christianitytoday.com/ct/1986/july-11/billy-graham-and-barefoot-evangelists.html

[2] https://billygrahamlibrary.org/amsterdam-1986-banner/

had prudently preserved legacies of the 17th-century Golden Age, such as the elaborate canal system artistically adorned with narrow yet ornate houses clad with gabled façades.

The city, heavily influenced by French culture, had a Baroque elegance reflected in the architecture of that period. There was also neo-classical style as well as Gothic structures. Over the years, several canals had been filled in, becoming streets or squares for shopping, residential and senior living communities. Yet, the charismatic heart of the city remained.

But for me, Amsterdam was a shock with its public cannabis smoking and other questionable activities that could buckle the nerves of any conservative American Christian in the 1980s.

De Wallen, better known as the red-light district, was built in medieval times at the city center—an intersection of channels and alleys with eclectic buildings used for dubious acts. Since 1811, the area had been designated for legal prostitution, regulated and taxed by the government. In 1911, it was prohibited but not eradicated, making a legal comeback in 2000. The scantily dressed women displayed behind wide glass windows of the small one-room apartments openly shopped their services, "the world's oldest profession."

Acknowledging this seedy side of Amsterdam's historical lexicon only made Billy Graham's event all the more poignant. What better place for a Christian convergence to learn and sharpen skills in combating iniquity.

Apart from its rambunctious nightlife, Amsterdam was ground zero for a prestigious collection of people and places who are rightfully honored with inspirational heritage sites and institutions. The Van Gogh Museum, the Rembrandt House Museum, the Anne Frank House, and the Royal Palace have their prominence among them.

The Conference for Itinerate Evangelists in Amsterdam

There was so much to take in. So many different kinds of people with varying perspectives, even regarding evangelism. This would prove to be a disappointing lesson, but one that serves me to this day.

Convenient Christianity

It was exciting to be where so many godly folks had gathered for this ten day coalition of like-minded, soul-supporting comrades.

Adding to the fun, I roomed with Cam Abell, a staff member of Harmony Bible Church in Danville, Iowa, whom I had met while on an outreach there the year before. We continued to bond during our time in the Netherlands. Like me, he was in his 30's, married, and had children. We talked in depth about ministry, evangelism, and scripture. I felt a genuine kinship and solidarity with him. We had the same love for expository preaching, and it was a great comfort to connect with someone who understood my passion. He was a true co-laborer in evangelizing the lost.

At the conference center each day—in the morning and at night—there was a main session that assembled for a message from Billy and/or one of his team members. As I sat a mere 100 feet from the pulpit, my view of things was both visually and spiritually awakening.

Joining Billy on stage was his son, Franklin (at the time, president of Samaritan's Purse), Argentinian evangelist Luis Palau, and Leighton Ford (the former VP of the Billy Graham Association but had recently left to start his own organization). Completing this crew of dynamo believers was worship leader Cliff Barrows and solo singer George Beverly Shea. Shea's rich, savory voice was a staple of Billy's globe-trotting crusades, and beloved by everyone who heard him.

By Shea's death in 2013, it was said by *The Washington Post* that his estimated audience of 220 million in a career spanning seven decades placed him as the most listened to artist in history.[3] This impressive team Billy had

---

3 https://www.washingtonpost.com/local/obituaries/george-beverly-shea-gospel-singer-who-preceded-billy-graham-sermons-dies-at-104/2013/04/17/4388e9a2-a77b-11e2-a8e2-5b98cb59187f_story.html

thoughtfully selected to surround himself with inspired me to do the same at EvanTell.

But what really struck me about Billy was his humility. It was a tangible symptom of Holy Spirit synergy. He and the Lord were not only collaborators; they were best friends, as we are all encouraged to be. What also inspired me was the way he kept promoting others and giving them the platform to speak. His drive to bring the gospel to the world (not just North Carolina) was never missing from his messages.

However, not everyone at the conference had such beliefs or practices.

After the main session, we would break into workshops with several hundred people in each. We took in lessons on every topic—speaking, character building, developing effective messages, traveling, and helping the local church foster evangelism in their own congregation.

All of this information was translated into twelve languages to accommodate the variety of nations represented there. But many of the attendees were away from their homeland for the first time. And due to their country's poverty level, living conditions, or civic unrest, a good number of them had no intention of leaving the Netherlands after the event was over.

With three quarters of the attendees traveling from third world countries, for many of them, the only reason they came to Amsterdam was to escape the hardship within their own nation. However, their return had been promised to their governments by the Billy Graham Association, and that promise was met. Still, so many of the documents dedicated to the visitors was printed in vain.

With this fact in mind, I met some evangelists who were missing the most important part of their Christian walk—a relationship with Christ. There was no meaning to the gospel truth, only words. One particular man I met from a developing nation, noticeably lacked this necessary element of faith.

"How did you come to know the Lord?" I asked him after a session one night.

He said that he had a "fearful experience" in the jungle, and that God had delivered him from it. That was it. His faith had nothing to do with Christ's sacrifice on the cross or being saved from an eternity without God. He was going on one experience where God rescued him from physical danger and his entire "Christian" walk was based on that alone.

So, I asked him, "If you could speak to God, and He asked you, 'Why should I let you into heaven?' what would you tell Him?"

He answered, "I've lived a good life and gone to church."

Then he told me of all the good things he had done—a virtual laundry list of deeds that would surely take him to heaven at the end of his life. No mention of why Jesus went to the cross and shed His blood on Calvary. In his mind, he had proven himself worthy of salvation on the grounds of his human actions.

But if he didn't know the heart of the gospel message, and yet called himself an evangelist, there was only one thing for me to do.

"Could I meet with you tomorrow, and show you in the Bible where it explains how you can know for certain that you're going to heaven?" I asked him.

He seemed agreeable, and we set a time and place to meet. I was eager to share what no doubt would change his entire perspective on how he taught the gospel. The next day, I sat waiting for him, but he never showed up. I can only assume that he was satisfied to be outside of his own country's border, and that the answer to the question about the assurance of heaven didn't interest him at all. He remained accountable to no one, and by his absence that day, he was happy with that arrangement.

How many other "Christians" at the event were basing their faith on convenience and not a Person—the One who died for them? How could they listen to inspirational words coming from Billy, Luis, Franklin, and others, and not care? The Way, the Truth, and the Life was available to them if they would open their heart to hear it and if God were to open their hearts to receive it. This made me even more committed to spreading the Truth in all its glory throughout the world.

Discovery in Disappointment

One of the final workshops I took was on developing an effective evangelistic message. It surprised and disappointed me to discover that they didn't begin with a specific scripture, as Dr. Robinson had taught me. Instead, they created a narrative that wasn't derived from a specific verse but gave an interesting story with scripture added to support it.

There was no careful study of verse(s) from which to develop a message. As it turned out, many of the evangelists I ran into did the opposite. I realized that knowing the difference (and practicing it myself) gave me an even clearer vision of my personal assignment and how to prepare to present the gospel to others.

At the end of our time in Amsterdam, Cam and I said our goodbyes, but would reunite the following year. He would join me at EvanTell helping to develop "N.E.T.S" (Non-threatening Evangelism Training System)—a three-month gospel-sharing training program based on Matthew 4:19, *"Follow me, and I will make you fishers of men."* This program was released in late summer of 1992 and became one of EvanTell's flagship products. Consisting of a twelve-part video series—a leader's manual and a student's manual—it was designed for the individual who had never led someone to Jesus Christ.

For eight years, Cam taught seminars, principally the *You Can Tell It!* sessions, occasionally travel with me, and aid in fine-tuning several aspects of the organization before moving to Richmond, Virginia, at the end of 1995 to be near family.

After the Amsterdam conference, I flew home to Dallas re-energized. However, still distressed at the notion that there were fellow evangelists traveling around, speaking to non-believers and seekers, all the while having no knowledge of the power of God's saving grace or Christ's role in the redemption story.

In September of 1986, I spoke at the Houston Chinese Church with the help of an interpreter. It was the first time I had actually worked in tandem with a translator. With approximately 300 in attendance, the parishioners were extremely receptive to the message. The practice of piggyback speaking was new to me, but one that I quickly caught on to. The last word from the interpreter was quickly followed by my next word—no lag time or awkward delays. It was fast and furious; quite a rush when we found our groove.

These international audiences were teaching me things that I could and would carry with me. However, there were three specific things I learned from Amsterdam that I would apply directly to EvanTell for its effectiveness and longevity.

First, I had a broader world vision for the ministry and its expansion. Secondly, I learned the importance of building a talented team around me. And finally, my experiences and conversations in the Netherlands reinforced my understanding for the need to create a ministry committed to the clarity of the gospel and the careful handling of scripture.

These truths would serve me well in the coming year when I would board another flight. This time, to the land of a million gods.

Nine

A Million Reasons to Go

O Death, where is your sting?
1 Corinthians 15:55a

Our plane touched down in New Delhi, India, in 1987—a land of humiliating poverty and an unforgiving caste system that flaunted the hierarchy within its complex culture. The humidity was relentless, even in January. Tammy and I met Ramesh Richard, the pastor of the host church, who took us to his home where we would stay during the five-day outreach. We left our son, David, with a trusted Christian couple that would care for him while we were away.

Hinduism, with its four major sects and what can amount to millions of gods and goddesses (depending on the sect), was overwhelming. Along with this highly charged spiritual environment, the natural surroundings were just as provoking with thick air pollution, scattered urban refuse, human excrement, and smoke from the dead rising from outdoor crematoriums that met my senses with a pulverizing jab.

There was a multitude of homeless people languishing on sidewalks, in street gutters, and train stations. The press of sweating bodies busy with their daily routines was like a river of flesh going over a dam in free fall—wet with perspiration, shining in the sun that beat down without pity. Then an unexpected downpour would darken the dust of souls ascending to the sky. This was India.

Following up with new converts from the India outreach

Nothing can truly prepare a westerner for the sights and smells of this South Asian country. With more than its share of deities and not nearly enough missionaries to serve the billion plus inhabitants, I was privileged to have been invited.

A Million Reasons to Go

The capital, New Delhi, is one of eleven districts within the city of Delhi, and home to a quarter of a million people at that time. However, the much larger metro area had a population of approximately 25 million—that was 18 million more than the Dallas-Fort Worth area, but only one-third of its geographical size.

Ramesh had a wife and small children. His house was located close to the church he pastored and where I would be speaking. This lovely family was kind and hospitable and made our stay a comfortable one.

I'm embarrassed to say that the lifestyles and practices of ordinary Indians, at first, shocked me. The burning of deceased bodies in plain view (a filthy job reserved for the "untouchables") carried the stench of death on the prevailing wind. People defecated in the streets. The crush of traffic was made worse by the lack of car lanes—people, automobiles, bikes, motorcycles, elephants, camels—all surged in one great disoriented caravan. You couldn't pay me to drive in India, despite a fervent prayer covering.

Among the local Indian preachers, the Rapture was described within a traffic joke: "The time between the light turning green and the first car honk," better known as "the twinkling of an eye." I guess aggravation and short tempers came with the territory in such cramped city limits. Even these men of God realized, after traveling abroad to westernized countries, India had a less than enviable transportation system.

I should mention that Hinduism is the major religion at 89% of New Delhi's population. What's left is a tiny percentage of communities made up of Muslims,

Christians, Sikhs, and Jains. And smaller still are groups of Parsis, Buddhists, and Jews.

A local custom of the Hindus was feeding the idols food offerings. I tried not to stare, but how does one hide the shock while watching the very faithful place precious food in the mouths of lifeless deities—cuisine any human being would be grateful to eat—only to have it clumsily fall back out? And these lovely dutiful people were calling the statues, "God." It was awkward and eerie how the effigies with their many arms, legs, and faces (half-animal / half-human) held such power. If the images weren't so disturbing, the situation could be laughable. But I was warned not to make light of it.

"Don't laugh or smile. This is serious," we were told. "The people will turn on you if they see you laughing." It was an offense Tammy and I made sure to avoid.

You might think that a land of a million gods would be the last place on earth anyone would want to learn about a single God who offered only one way to heaven. But I think that was my initial draw to India. The Hindus are extremely devoted to their religion, their many gods, and to their rituals.

For instance, the Ganges River that runs through Delhi is the center of an annual mass pilgrimage for Hindus from all over the country. Bathing in the river signifies spiritual purification—washing away of sins. It's a yearly spectacle with its throng wrapped in colorful cloth, praying pilgrims splashing in the water, and the soft glow of candles floating on the current at dusk. Some folks will collect water in jars and carry it home (hundreds of miles away) to friends and family unable to make the journey.

Looking around me, I considered the United States where there were Christians who refused to go even a mile to their local church on a Sunday morning. It gave me compassion for the Indian people who served their gods in complete loyalty and love. And it gave me hope that they would receive the one true God with the same vitality and commitment.

Christian workers I trained in evangelism in India

The outreach sponsored by Ramesh's church, Delhi Bible Fellowship—the largest church in northern India—brought in hundreds searching for the truth about Jesus Christ. I was thankful for my previous experience working with an interpreter at the Chinese church in Houston, so things went smoothly. It was such a success that Ramesh invited me back in 1990 for a city-wide outreach, and also to teach on how to effectively share the good news of the gospel. Upon my return there, I found the poverty, lack of sanitation, and overpopulation still prevalent. But the people's eagerness to learn, to worship, and to pray had multiplied.

Directly related to that visit, I received a letter in 2021 from a man who attended the New Deli outreach in 1990. In part, it read:

"I know you will not be able to remember me, but you are always remembered by me. I came to know the Lord in New Delhi in 1987 after attending one of the evening outreaches at Delhi Bible Fellowship. One evening, I met you at the door and asked you, "How could one be sure of forgiveness from God?" You were in a hurry for Pastor Ramesh Richard and others were waiting for you. But you took the time and pointed out John 5:24 and read it to me. That was enough. I went out and read that verse and started reading the whole Book of John before that Sunday evening meeting at DF. Since then, I am convinced that anything concerning God and Man is revealed in the Word of God. The Lord has given me many brothers and sisters in Christ, and I'm enjoying Him and His people's fellowship. Thank you for being faithful to the Lord in witnessing to me. I remember Pastor Ramesh jokingly saying that your wife—who sang that day—sings like a nightingale, and you, like a nightmare. Nevertheless, John 5:24 was wonderful. Thanks, and may the Lord bless you, your family, and your ministry."

If ever there was a reason to go halfway around the world, that was it in a nutshell. It's what I had spent years training for, and it was a sweet reward for that labor. It was definite evidence that God was working through me, and it filled my heart with deep humility and gratitude.

Preaching the gospel through an interpreter at the Delhi, India outreach

After the 1987 outreach in New Delhi, Tammy and I flew south to Bangalore, India, a teeming city with a population of twelve million. The timing couldn't have been better since I would already be in the country and was able to secure transportation to the area. It was a long and exhausting trip, with as many potholes as there were mosquitoes. For the next two days, I taught at the Asian Christian Academy on the topic of evangelistic preaching.

The invitation came from Dr. Joy George, the head of the academy. This opportunity would expose fifty pastoral students of all ages to the expository evangelism training I passionately shared.

My wife and I stayed in a modest room at the academy designated for visiting professors. Its concrete floors, plain walls, and simple beds were reminiscent of the basic living quarters of missionaries throughout the world in centuries past.

As Jesus said, "Foxes have holes and birds of the air have nests, but the Son of man has nowhere to lay His head" (Matthew 8:20). It seemed only fitting that Christ's servants would need little else than four walls, a roof, and a bed (if that much) to spread His message of salvation. When there are so many people hungry for the Word of God, as these academic students were, fine décor and creature comforts would hardly add to the abundant riches found in Christ.

At the end of our trip to India, Tammy and I returned to Dallas with a wider view of the world. There was a spiritual darkness in places around the globe where Christ was urgently needed. I had seen firsthand a new kind of spiritual wilderness. It cried out to me, and I was answering that call.

But now, I was home—home in the U.S. with common luxuries like clean air, orderly streets, and a church on every corner. Sanitary water and government inspected food. And the cemeteries with their manicured lawns, free of the foul smell of smoke with just rows of fresh flowers left beside polished headstones . . . and one with a familiar name.

A Million Reasons to Go

Mourning and Evening

The dairy cows, the barn and buildings, the nearby woods, and my childhood farmhouse—it was all still there. When I was away at college, Johnny married a sweet gal named Velma, and they had three amazing kids: Diane, Carol, and Brenda. Johnny bought a home that nuzzled against my parents' property—perfect for his budding family.

But unforeseen events can come rushing in without permission, troubling the placid water of life as we know it. Like an avalanche that crashes down a mountainside, on July 14, 1982, at the age of thirty-eight, Velma died of a blood clot, leaving Johnny with the children, now eight, twelve, and thirteen. Bless my parents for their love and support during that somber time.

A couple of years later, Mom and Dad also purchased a house next to the farm and moved in when Dad retired. He found great pleasure gazing out of the window to see his oldest son working the same fields that he did as a young man. The few occasions when Johnny needed help, Dad was quick to step up and lend a hand. But for the most part, my brother had taken the reins and was now in charge of the business.

In his tumultuous teens, Johnny dropped out of high school, thinking it was a worthless endeavor when it came to his blue collar, labor-dominated farm job. He also made no apology for his opinion that college students were lazy. Knowing my strong work ethic though, he never accused me of that. I could tell though that he struggled at times with me going to Philadelphia College of Bible and Dallas Seminary. He just couldn't understand how Mom and Dad could spend hard-earned money on books when there was always farm equipment to buy. But over the years, Johnny came to appreciate what I had accomplished, supported me wholeheartedly, and that made me smile.

Johnny and Velma and Tammy and I found a relaxed equilibrium between us, which included casual dinners together at their home when we visited during the holidays. As couples, we had become close, finding a calm maturity as we left youth's insecurities and grudges behind.

When Velma died, Johnny's depression is probably what led to a delinquent diet and excessive weight gain, which put him over three-hundred pounds. Because of it, his health suffered. Still, it never kept him from his duties on the farm.

About two years after his wife passed, Johnny met Shirley and they were married. Soon, a baby boy named Paul (lovingly called "PJ") joined the ranks of the Moyer clan.

It seemed that Johnny and I had found a beautiful stability in our lives that reached into every area—spouse, children, business. Everything we dreamed of having and worked so hard for had come to fruition. I wasn't aware of Johnny's concerns about the farm and its viability over the long haul. My brother was incredibly talented with machines, but not so gifted in finance. None of us realized the stress he was under as he tried to keep the farm afloat.

Due to some questionable business decisions he had made, pressure was building until his body reached a breaking point on September 23, 1987.

I suspect that Wednesday was like any other day when Johnny got up in the morning. About noon, he had lunch with his oldest daughter at the diner where she worked as a waitress. Diane was 18 years old and just getting her feet wet in the world. They enjoyed some father-daughter time over a meal and then said their goodbyes. She went off to meet her boyfriend for a fun afternoon of fishing. Johnny told Diane that he would see her at home later.

When my brother got back to the farmhouse, he began to experience pain in his chest.

"It's probably just indigestion," he told Shirley.

He then collapsed to the floor and went into full cardiac arrest. Shirley quickly dialed 911, then waited for the EMTs to arrive. In the 1980s, performing CPR wasn't common knowledge to lay people, and all Shirley could do in her state of panic was hold him and wait. When the emergency workers got there, they tried to revive him, but it was too late. Johnny died from a "widowmaker" at the age of forty-six on the sofa of our family farmhouse.

It was unthinkable.

My sister was the one who broke the news to my parents. She then called me at EvanTell.

Though Lorraine was my twin, we rarely spoke over the phone long distance. When I heard her voice on the other end, I knew something was desperately wrong.

"Larry, I have some bad news," her stoic voice said.

I immediately thought that Dad or Mom had died.

"It's Johnny," she continued, "it looks like he died from a heart attack."

"What! When?" I couldn't wrap my mind around it. This was my big brother. He was always going to be there. He couldn't possibly be dead.

It was the previous fall when I last saw Johnny. Yes, we chose different paths. I went down the academic road while he stayed home to work with his hands. My thoughts were of traveling the world; his were grounded in the land and the family dynasty. But he loved me, and I loved him. Sibling rivalry had at last faded. *How could he be gone?*

"It just happened," Lorraine's words pulled me back to the present. "We'll let you know when the funeral is."

"I'm scheduled to be in Sunbury this weekend," I answered.

The call was short, and suddenly it was over, and I was left stunned and heartbroken. Denial pleaded with me to forget what I had just heard, but the truth can't be silenced, just as the pain is still easily recalled so many decades later. I feel it even now. I called my folks and, understandably, they could hardly talk in the midst of their grief.

Sunbury, Pennsylvania, was a little town just seventy-five miles from Elizabethtown, and I couldn't help but think about God's sovereignty as it covered this implausible situation. My plane ticket was already purchased for a speaking engagement on Sunday. It was now Wednesday.

My brain jumbled with questions. How were my parents going to handle this, and what would happen to the farm? Johnny kept their dream alive running things. My parents had only been living in their new home for six months. How were the children going to fare? Who was going to look after them? Three girls left behind, ages eighteen, seventeen, thirteen, and a two-year-old little boy. How would everyone cope with such a devastating loss?

But like always, my parents took on the challenge much like any other—with a steel spine not easily broken. They helped raise their granddaughters while Shirley cared for baby PJ.

Over one hundred people attended Johnny's funeral, mostly family and farm friends. Mom and Dad were devastated, and sorrow gripped their faces, refusing to let go. Shirley was inconsolable while the kids stared blankly with pooling eyes, anguish seeping out with every tear. We were all just hanging on.

The service lasted about an hour, and my thoughts wandered off to the woods, hills, and back country where Johnny and I stalked game together. I thought about his chainsaw accident, and also his fury the time our cat, Tippy, was killed. Snapshots of our shared lives ran through my mind as the local pastor's voice laid down a poor soundtrack for such meaningful memories.

Not long before his death, Johnny had begun to drive the bus for a nearby church, and even went forward to make his faith public. Because of a talk Tammy and I had with him over dinner a couple of years earlier, I wasn't worried about his salvation, only for the suffering of my folks, his children and grieving wife.

Being a preacher myself, and an evangelist, I yearned to say just a few words over my brother's coffin, but that wasn't permitted by the liberal church my family attended. Only the serving pastor was allowed to address the mourners in the dogmatic, ritualistic ceremony.

It seemed absurd that the pastor didn't offer any message of the gospel, only stories about his own personal life and pastoring with a hint of self-importance. Like week-old bread on the shelf of a four-star bistro, this same man who was known for telling inappropriate jokes around town was now presiding over my brother's funeral. I wasn't really surprised at his tone deaf and self-centered approach. But I hated that it was a wasted opportunity—those present wouldn't hear a message about Christ's forgiveness and redemption.

When the service was over, family and close friends drove to the Maytown Union Cemetery for the burial, just outside of Elizabethtown. The day was mostly overcast with occasional sun peeking through the clouds as if to say that things would get brighter at some point. Just not all at once.

After the burial, Tammy and I hugged Mom and Dad, and traveled just over an hour to Sunbury for my speaking engagement. Four days after my brother passed, I was ministering to a church congregation looking to me for reassurance and hope. Sometimes, God uses a moment where we are completely drained. He empties us of ourselves in order to give His very best. I can only hope that His words were heard and not my own.

We flew home to Dallas several days later.

Heaven Has Them

One month after Johnny's death, Dad had a heart attack but made it through. A few months later in January of 1988, Mom suffered an aneurysm of the aorta and lost one kidney. But she lived. During that time of recovery, a local minister visited my parents and they talked to him about their grief, their faith, and the afterlife.

It seems ironic that their evangelist son wasn't the one God used to bring about their conversations, but honestly, it makes sense. My family was notorious for never talking to each other about such things. But as my folks spoke to this local pastor, they assured him of their salvation. And Mom made a special point of telling me so when I saw her the following month in February.

On February 28, my dear dad departed for heaven. Some say he died of a broken heart, and I wouldn't disagree. I truly believe that losing Johnny was simply too much for him to bear. He cried every day after Johnny was gone. He missed him every minute. So, five months after putting his oldest son to rest, Dad joined him.

After Dad's death, my mother moved in with my sister, Lorraine, who never married. With one kidney lost, her health was failing. She was, in her last days, transferred to an assisted living facility. Sadly, there is little that can be done for end-stage renal disease, and she was left with two grim choices: dialysis or death.

She chose the latter.

Tammy, David, and I came into town and stayed with Lorraine. My visit with Mom was, in many ways, difficult due to her failing health. But she was the woman with qualities I always hoped to find in my future wife. Fortunately for me, that ideal was made real in Tammy.

I was told Mom died right after I left. No one was with her when she passed.

It had been eight years without Johnny or Dad when Mom was finally laid to rest in January of 1996 at the age of eighty-two. The night before, a tempestuous blizzard had blown through Elizabethtown, leaving a deep blanket of snow now piled high on the roads and hills. A snowplow cleared a path to the cemetery. The funeral procession slowly crept into the graveyard, inching forward and finally sliding to a stop.

Next to my father's burial plot was another, open and waiting, for Mom to take her place beside him.

After the service and burial, we drove down the lane hemmed in on each side by a brash bank of snow, and I thought about the path we walk in following Jesus. In places it may look dangerous—a slippery slope where progress is slow. But Jesus has cleared the way ahead of us, and all we need do is trust Him.

Then I heard Mom's voice as I remembered a past conversation we'd had about the local pastor who visited her and Dad after Johnny's death. The discussion I always longed to have with them, but never did, gave me peace. She made a point to tell me, "Larry, you've always been concerned about our salvation, but you don't have to worry anymore." Although they found it hard to talk about, she assured me that both of them understood the gospel and the purpose of His sacrificial death. My concern expressed even through a letter had not been in vain.

The tires slid slightly, the ice shined like glass, and then the sun came out.

A Million Reasons to Stay

When I look back on my own life, I imagine that there are a million different reasons to go be with the Lord, then another million reasons to stay. Our body is made of dust, like the earth, and we feel our connection to it. I can stand in a muddy field as rain gently falls and feel at one with the animals and nature God has provided for my pleasure and stewardship.

Our loved ones are here with us on this sentimental blue ball, cradling our dreams and encouraging our souls. And we cannot forget that the Holy Spirit is here, guiding and girding us up on our quest to spread the gospel.

For now, I'm still here, though in the twilight of my life with "winter upon my head," as Victor Hugo so eloquently put it. For me, the North Star shines as brightly as it ever has. My hunger to reach as many people as possible with the good news of the gospel has never dimmed. My journey on earth will, one day, come to an end. But like so many faithful Christians who have gone before me, what follows will more than atone for the aching heart that I have carried here on earth.

Ten

Winds of Change

Jesus Christ is the same yesterday, today, and forever.
Hebrews 13:8

A season of growth was upon EvanTell and in the summer of 1989 we moved into a bigger office facility to accommodate our vision of expansion.

The following year, we hired an auditing service to demonstrate the ministry's financial transparency and to prove its priority of integrity. Board members were delighted to hear from the auditor, "We work with fifteen to twenty different nonprofits and would put EvanTell at the top for its financial management and accountability. The record keeping and ethical standards serve as an example to other organizations." We had successfully met our godly intentions, practicing vigilance in our bookkeeping in order to balance every penny spent.

EvanTell had been in existence for nearly twenty years, and we remained alert and responsible for the funds that God provided, and the outreaches that ministered to thousands of people. Because of our desire to be a company beyond reproach, EvanTell became a member of the Evangelical Council of Financial Accountability—the Better Business Bureau of the Christian world. As a "watchdog," ECFA upholds the highest ethical standards for the Christian business community, and it was an honor to be recognized and brought under the umbrella of such a trusted organization.

So many wonderful things were happening at the turn of the decade. In May of 1990, I was invited to be a weekly regular on a national talk show. Don Hawkins, the host of "Life Perspectives," which broadcasted from Dallas, aired on sixty stations throughout the country. He fielded questions from callers about God, their faith and/or doubts, and challenging issues on Christian subjects. Pretty soon, there were so many people calling in that there wasn't enough time for me to speak to everyone.

Like a holy wind that swept in, from the plains to the Rocky Mountains, the calls kept coming. One evening, a man named Perry phoned from Wisconsin. Listening to him, I realized he didn't understand the gospel and he confessed that he wasn't sure that he would go to heaven when he died. For me, there's nothing that gets my adrenaline pumping faster than someone who is open to hearing the gospel. This is what transpired on that night as several thousand people listened.

As I carefully explained the Bad News/Good News to him, he quietly absorbed all that I said. And when I had finished laying out the gospel message in the clearest terms possible, I explained a concept that few people trusting the Lord ever hear.

I said, "Saying a prayer doesn't save you. It's trusting Christ that saves you. But if right now, you want to place your trust in Christ, here is how you can tell God what you are doing. Repeat these words after me, *Dear God, I'm a sinner.*"

"Dear God, I'm a sinner," Perry declared, repeating each word I said. Full-throated from his lips to God's ears, he continued to repeat after me. "I now understand that nothing I do will get me to heaven. But I also understand that Jesus Christ died for me and that He rose again. And right now, I'm trusting Jesus alone as my only way to heaven. Thank you for the free gift of eternal life that I just received. In Jesus' name, amen."

To ensure that Perry completely understood everything that he had just said, I asked two of the most important questions there are.

"Where would you go if you died right now?"

"I would go to heaven," Perry answered.

"And if you stood before God and He asked you, 'Why should I let you into heaven?' what would you tell Him?"

"Because I trusted Christ," he said, unabashedly knowing and believing all that it meant.

There it was. He understood what had just occurred when he made the decision to trust Christ. From that night on, I would learn that Perry was discipled by another believer and continued to have a tremendous testimony and impact upon his family and friends.

The power of God is not merely words; it's our faith in action. Yes, we pray with language, and He hears us. But the Holy Spirit also speaks for us when words escape us. "The Spirit Himself makes intercession for us with groanings which cannot be uttered" (Roman 8:26b). It's not our eloquence or fancy vocabulary that God notices. It's not the number of words we say or repeat. It is the mountain-moving faith in Christ and His sacrifice on a cross that saves us.

Love beyond words.

Evangelism Reinvented

In January of 1992, I found myself back in Amsterdam, teaching thirty students the skills of expository evangelism. Since this paradigm wasn't being taught at the college, Tyndale invited me to come and give a weeklong tutorial. Without Tammy with me, I stayed on campus grounds in a room the school graciously provided. The international students were incredibly grateful that I flew so far to teach such a small number of them. As there wasn't access to this kind of teaching in their home countries, they had to leave their own land and come to a place like Tyndale Seminary in order to gain that kind of training.

When the week was over, I left encouraged by the quality of Christians devoting their lives to the advancement of the gospel.

Being there in the Netherlands again brought back memories of the Billy Graham conference, my time with great friend (and now co-worker at EvanTell) Cam Abell, and my shared experiences with evangelists from all corners of the globe. It had become apparent that my passion for evangelism was ready for a wider net, an outreach program to broaden EvanTell's services.

For this, I would need someone to help me coordinate the effort.

Warren Hunt was a humble man that I had met in 1988 when I spoke at the First Baptist Church in League City, Texas, where he served as Minister of Music. We worked together again in July of 1990 at an outreach in Mississippi. Not only did Warren have exceptional abilities, but he was someone sensitive to non-believers, as well as a team player who exalted Jesus, not himself.

Warren was as sincere in his faith as anyone could be. His personal character and caliber of moral conduct was a perfect fit for the ministry and aligned with my own walk and way of presenting the Word of God. He joined EvanTell in the spring of 1991 as the soloist, song leader, and event coordinator to help organize the outreaches.

As EvanTell moved forward, our "Purpose and Vision Statement" was finalized, highlighting three features that best reflected the ministry's objectives: to reach, teach, and equip. Our outreaches and conferences were designed to *reach* as many people as possible. Our seminars would *teach* the gospel in clear and certain terms. And this knowledge would *equip* Christians to spread the gospel far and wide.

The recalibration of the inner workings of EvanTell brought greater success in tandem with two new seminars implemented in 1993. They were *You Can Preach It!*—expository preaching tools for pastors, evangelists, and church leaders; and *You Can Tell It!*—designed to develop personal evangelism skills for lay leaders or any believer with a heart for spreading the gospel. Cam Abell loved teaching the *You Can Tell it!* seminar and was so gifted at it.

After Cam's departure from the ministry, it was no longer deemed best to have only one person serving as the *You Can Tell It!* instructor. Soon, it was set up as an institute, and individuals could gain certification to teach the material. It was a sound decision in order to spread this valuable information for others to teach.

About the same time, being the President and CEO, the Chairman of the Board and I recognized that EvanTell's Board of Directors needed the benefit of individuals with an intense resolve to advance the ministry and also the time in their own schedules to serve effectively. To meet those ends, a list of responsibilities was drawn up in a document that each board member would agree to fulfill.

The board also increased its membership from six to twelve. Dr. Haddon Robinson remained on the board, and additional associates experienced in leadership who would give generously of their time and energy would grow EvanTell to its full potential.

Individuals came on board to assist in product development, formulating a product list, assisting in getting our Non-Threatening Evangelism Training System off the ground, and doing extensive promotion. It was a decisive moment—we needed to do something to ensure the growth and longevity of this essential global ministry. God continued to amaze me, bringing the right people into the organization at just the right time.

In 1995, I realized I could no longer feasibly keep up with the day-to-day operations of EvanTell. I also realized that my focus on administration wasn't a wise use of my time and ability. Fred Sewell, a businessman who greatly ministered to me would always ask, "What are you doing that someone else could do—to free you up to do what *they* can't do?" To thoughtfully delegate responsibilities made good sense, so I restructured the ministry once again to designate a new position. A Director of Operations would oversee the daily functions of the ministry.

In a historic six-hour meeting between the Associate Evangelist, Cam Abell, the Program Director, Warren Hunt, as well as myself, we discussed the outreach events, our methodology of communicating the gospel, and what we could do to extend the outreach of the ministry. If the entire world were to be reached, we had to evolve and change with the culture.

The information coming from church leaders regarding the *You Can Tell It!* seminar was exciting. The outreaches were consistently producing passionate believers willing to step out of their usual comfort zones to speak to non-believers, thus fueling the cycle of evangelism.

A Table of Friends

The message will never change, but the method has to. That was a notion that loomed in the back of my mind as the years went on. Toward Billy Graham's retirement, he realized that evangelism needed to evolve in order to address the dwindling numbers of unbelievers attending his crusades. Christians continued to attend, but non-believers weren't coming in the proportion they were years earlier.

I also noticed a shift in the air when it came to active Christianity. It was becoming more difficult getting people to attend an outreach on a weeknight. And it was even more challenging to bring in non-believers to church on a Sunday morning. We needed to acclimate to the changing social environment if evangelism was to survive.

With twenty years of ministry under my belt, I was convinced that though the gospel message never changes, my approach had to if EvanTell was to endure. It was then that I decided to incorporate a radical approach, offering a brand new format: a weekend-long outreach called Operation Friendship. Promoted nationwide and in Canada, churches would advertise the event as a "friendship dinner" with a discussion on salvation and heaven.

My requirement for a church to participate never depended on the size of the church or its financial resources. The church only had to meet two criteria in order for me to come: they had to *pray* and *promote*. That is, to schedule the date and get the word out, and to steadfastly cover it in prayer. Though it was never a consideration for me to decline any invitation due to the projected turnout, attendees usually numbered anywhere from fifty to five hundred people. Couples usually brought other couples; singles brought singles.

Sponsored by a local church, their members would bring non-Christian friends to a lovely formal dinner at a restaurant or hotel for an evening of food, fellowship, and conversation focused on topics centered on Christ and why He is the way to heaven. The relaxed atmosphere welcomed the faithfully committed but, more importantly, it also welcomed the spiritually curious.

Most Operation Friendships averaged 40% non-Christians

Guests ate a scrumptious meal while they listened to a music program—inspirational secular songs and spiritual songs such as *Amazing Grace*. This introduced a church member that would share their testimony before I would give the message. Not a conventional church service message, but probing questions to intrigue and engage those sitting on the fence of their faith.

What does God say about our mistakes and failures of the past?

If God had 5 minutes with you, what would He want to tell you?

Since the Bible is so confusing, is there anything in it that *everyone* can understand?

If 10 different people give you 10 different ways to heaven, how do you know who's right?

If Christians are hypocrites and churches are boring, why would anyone consider Christ?

These questions allowed me to fill in many of the blind spots that non-believers struggle with in their quest to find the truth. On one occasion, a Christian brought twenty-six unbelievers with him. The highest proportion of non-believers recorded, that I know of, was 60% due to the pastor's personal outreach and invitations.

At the end of the dinner, I would invite folks to put their trust in Christ—right then and there. Everybody got a communication card to share their name, address, age, and who invited them. This would help to expedite the local church's follow-up. And on the card was a box indicating whether they came to Christ that night.

Sunday morning, the guests would come to the host church for an evangelistic service, and a one-hour mini-seminar later that night on the topic of evangelism.

Since the time we implemented Operation Friendship, it has been instrumental in EvanTell moving outward to reach more people than ever before. There is a story of a couple who had their lives changed by one such dinner, that I'd like to share with you now.

A Friend at the Table

Katy and Mark were members of the Jenison Bible Church in Hudsonville, Michigan. When they decided to attend a Friendship Dinner, they prayerfully invited a young couple that Katy knew. Janice and Jaden committed to come but would need to find someone to look after their one-year-old little boy. Katy and Mark thanked the Lord for opening that door and asked others to join them in prayer for the non-Christian couple.

Restaurants offered a good setting for an after-dinner message

On the night of the dinner, Janice and Jaden canceled, and left Katy and Mark disappointed, but trusting that

God has a reason for everything. They believed that He had another couple in mind. The Spirit led them to an employee of Mark's named Steven, and his girlfriend Lonnie, whom they had been praying for.

Two months before, when Steven had accidentally locked himself out of his apartment, a new tenant saw him apparently breaking in and called the police. Steven was quickly arrested when their background check revealed his previous record, which included a warrant for delinquent child support. Due to a stretch of unemployment, he simply couldn't pay the determined amount. Steven had just started working for Mark when the authorities took him to jail.

While Steven was incarcerated, his heart softened as he realized his life needed to change. Three days before the Friendship Dinner, Steven was released.

But when Katy and Mark called to extend the invitation to the event, he had a new unlisted number. The clock was ticking, and the couple started to doubt that things would come together in time. Then Katy remembered the name of Lonnie's sister, and through divine channels, they were able to contact Steven and Lonnie and invite them to the banquet. And they agreed to come!

The couple was seated in front where Mark and Katy knew there would be few distractions. As they listened to my message Lonnie and Steven held each other's hand tightly.

When it was time to fill out the communication card, Mark began to pray. In the past, Christians had been accusatory and judgmental toward Steven, which kept him from seeking God. As he was writing, Katy squeezed

Mark's leg. The young man had checked his card indicating that he had made a decision to trust Jesus. Though Steven didn't verbally share what he did, he made his card clearly visible for them to see.

It was the perfect time, place, and opportunity Steven needed to come to Christ.

After that night, Katy and Mark continued to ask God to use them in encouraging and guiding Steven and Lonnie, helping them to grow in their faith.

And what of the couple, Janice and Jaden, that had canceled at the last minute? It was a short time later when Katy received a call from Janice, which would confirm God's will and ways are known only to Him. Janice told her that she had been in a horrific auto accident—a rollover landing the car upside down in a ditch. Miraculously, she walked away unharmed, but the crash left her terrified.

"Katy, I was so scared. I truly thought I was going to die. What would have happened to my child if I didn't make it!?"

"More importantly, Janice, what would have happened to *you* if you had died?" Katy responded. "Can you honestly tell me where you would be spending eternity?" The silence on the other end answered her question.

Then Katy shared the Bad News/Good News with Janice, and when she was finished, her friend was crying. She confessed that she now wanted to trust Jesus Christ as her only way to heaven.

Exactly one week later, Janice collapsed in her home. She was rushed to the hospital where she died soon after that of kidney failure. Unbeknownst to her, she had been stricken with a kidney disease and was living on borrowed time. She left a baby boy not yet two years old and a devastated husband who was now forced to create a future without her.

Janice's funeral would follow days later, and Katy prayed that she would have the boldness to share the gospel with Jaden.

This testimony emphasizes that our time on earth is not guaranteed. It is limited and fleeting and filled with unknowns. It is a mist that drifts across the ground for a moment, then vanishes in the sunlight. Like the wind, it is invisible but durable, until it's gone. It can change direction in an instant, leaving us disheveled and awestruck at its unpredictability. It is a joyful mystery.

May we all be aware of those around us and seize every opportunity to offer hope for the future, forgiveness for the past, and a heavenly home with God forever.

Eleven

Expeditions in the Western Hemisphere

How then shall they call on Him in whom they have not believed? And how shall they believe in Him of whom they have not heard? And how shall they hear without a preacher?
Romans 10:14

Growing up, I often heard children's laughter. Then one day, it dawned on me that they were laughing at me, usually when I spoke. Some words came easily for me while others caught in my mouth—like the rabbits I used to hunt that would tangle up in a thicket, spinning and struggling to get out. Still, I could sense that my entire life—short or long—would be dedicated to preaching. As I've shared earlier, then a doctor said the cruelest thing of all.

"Too bad you're never going to be a speaker with your problem."

Those careless words directed at an impressionable child were no match for God. "Being confident of this very thing, that He who began a good work in you will complete it until the day of Jesus Christ" (Philippians 1:6). The way I saw it, God had already made up His mind. I was destined to talk about Him to others.

A challenging speech impediment from a very young age would have, for many, canceled that dream and extinguished any hope of a future in evangelism. But in God's economy, our lack is His fortune! It is in our own brokenness that we are perfectly fitted to accomplish His seemingly impossible will.

If someone would have told me in the beginning that I would, one day, be a globe-trotting evangelist, I would have believed them blindly. Who better for God to send out to reveal His power, grace, and goodness than the most unlikely person? For it is not me who is speaking, but God speaking through me.

I've enjoyed every minute of my travels and meeting people of other races and nationalities. Lodging with host pastors and their families has allowed me to connect on a very personal level. It also brings accountability, in that there is someone always present to see that my actions and behavior are equal to my post. And it's also a great way to gauge the temperature of the community.

The next two chapters are devoted to my journeys to other countries, teaching, preaching, and sharing the gospel. In every place, I was being used by God to reach the lost or to train believers in evangelism and was often doing both. I trust that they will provide insight into the cultures I've experienced and bring clarity (and perhaps inspiration) to those who feel a yearning to forge their own path in sharing the good news off the beaten trail.

Haiti had nearly seven million inhabitants in 1989 when I was there for a weeklong outreach. I found the 90% unemployment rate startling. Peoples' average annual income was $380 and four out of five people were illiterate. When an underdeveloped country lacks the ability to maintain its citizens with its own resources—those things which support quality of life—it relies heavily on outside help. But as important as the people's material needs were, their need for spiritual health was even greater.

The environment was extreme. With rice as the main food source, occasionally the lack of red meat would induce some to kill a cat for a meal. The shanty towns with houses separated only by flimsy curtains made it difficult to assess just how many family members shared a single dwelling.

In the face of such destitution, the locals believed that if they made friends with a visiting American, financial support for them and their family could be forthcoming. This created a surge of attention toward us, which helped in our outreach efforts.

It was the middle of sultry summer when I flew into Port-au-Prince to stay with a U.S. missionary. Coming from Texas, I quickly acclimated to the wilting heat and humidity. We took a smaller plane to visit several other places on the island, Pignon and Pétion-Ville among them, but afterward we always returned to the missionary's home in Port-au-Prince. The time I spent there went swiftly, and before I knew it, I was in Dallas again. However, word got back to us that thousands had listened to the outreach via radio, and many of them came to Christ.

Preaching the gospel at the Haiti outreach

When I left Haiti, I was saddened that I wasn't a millionaire. If only I had enough money, I could assist them financially. But I was thrilled I told thousands of folks about something more valuable than money—the treasure that comes from knowing Jesus Christ.

In a place where there is great need, there is also great opportunity.

Havana, Cuba, was the destination for a research expedition—an observation and note-taking trip for future ministry. EvanTell's major tract, *May I Ask You* *a Question?* had been so well-received that prior to my coming I was told that the excitement was palpable. I would also discover just how impactful the material from our ministry had been.

This communist-led country exercised an intimidating chokehold on its people and wore a poor disguise of faux freedom—a façade for foreign visitors on vacation or there on business. It was for that reason, and only that reason, our material was allowed in.

Cuba was frozen in the 1950's with antique cars still running via repurposed parts, and weather-worn buildings in desperate need of a fresh coat of paint. With people so oppressed under an authoritarian regime, a person could get arrested for openly expressing his or her opinions, especially if those ideas opposed the methods of the government.

They could be detained and imprisoned for speaking their minds, preaching a doctrine, or publicly airing grievances contrary to the administration's position. There was a casual caution exercised by its citizens, and not a hint of discontent was heard. Raúl Castro (the younger brother of Fidel) was in power and directing the United Party of the Socialist Revolution of Cuba (PURSC), which took over in 1965. The Communist Party of Cuba rules to this day.

A Christian worker with a local church was kind enough to take me on a tour of some historical sites, such as Revolutionary Square, formerly called Plaza Cívica, where the revolutionary rallies started Fidel Castro's takeover.

An ominous scene was a Cold War staging area for what would be known as the Cuban Missile Crisis. From a distance, I could see where the Russian and Cuban armies had set up blockades for the interception of U.S. ships—giving the USSR strategic access to the southern coast of the United States. But thankfully in 1962, John F. Kennedy successfully averted a catastrophe, and we maintained our national security.

But despite its tumultuous past and impeded present, I felt optimistic seeing how zealous the community was for spiritual things. I discovered an abundance of "house churches" threaded throughout the neighborhoods, which gave people (many without transportation) places to worship. And it was EvanTell's material that helped equip those pastors and church leaders.

I was hoping that our ministry would create real change there. Sadly, just after we left, the Covid-19 virus hit, and all of our carefully laid plans for the coming year were canceled.

Mexico City came with a warning: "Watch out whose car you get into at the airport. And don't believe what anyone tells you, since there's a good chance they may be attempting to kidnap you." The uncomfortable reality was that Americans were known to disappear since they were targeted for their monetary wealth and connections.

With that bit of unsettling information, I was picked up by the host missionary. From there we were off to Pachuca, about fifty-six miles away, where I spent the majority of my time as I taught our *You Can Tell It!* seminar. Though deemed safer than Mexico City, I was still cautioned about where I could go.

Preaching through an interpreter in Mexico

The spiritual zeal of the locals was only matched by the soaring crime rate. I was advised where *not* to take my morning run, because I would return with no shoes. Even the police were corrupt and supported the criminals for a share of their dark earnings.

Finished in Pachuca, I traveled back to Mexico City and its 8.5 million residents for another speaking engagement before flying out the next day—shoes intact. I'm happy to report that EvanTell continues to have a strong presence in Mexico through our contract workers.

El Salvador, known as the Land of Volcanos, is the smallest country in Central America.

The poverty has dropped over time, but the number of poor per capita was still significantly higher than other places I had traveled. While not on the list of impoverished nations in that area, it is still considered "third world" with limited resources and an elevated crime rate.

The food, as you can imagine, was delicious. Handmade tortillas, tamales, and a variety of exotic fruits were in abundance. When spending time in the city, we ate robust beef, tender pork, and roasted chicken. In coastal towns, fresh fish with rice was served, staples on just about every table.

For eight days, I taught evangelistic preaching to pastors in the towns of San Miguel, San Salvador, and Santa Ana. That covered the east, central and western parts of El Salvador. It was Jim Adams, a missionary with CAM International, who invited me there, and also chauffeured us from place to place. A servant's heart and a common goal bound us together in our love for Christ.

The attendees of the *You Can Preach It!* seminar were friendly and received the training eagerly. My hope was that it would dramatically affect how those pastors preached, as they had a tendency to talk for hours without any deliberate preconceived message. Never having been taught how to develop a sermon from biblical text, they just talked. The training they received from EvanTell was indispensable to changing that mindset and practice.

Brazil is a breathtaking place of fruit and nut trees, clusters of bright yellow flowers of the Cassia leptophylla bending its branches, swaying palms, and clouds heavy with rain. It all captured my imagination in vivid technicolor. And swirled into the beauty of the tropical landscape was a population living in squalor—an unharmonious mixture of paradise and poverty.

Brazilian students receiving training in evangelism

In Atibaia, Brazil, I spoke at a local church under the umbrella of the Word of Life Bible Institute. It was there that one of the local pastors said to me, "The reason people in Brazil don't evangelize is the same reason in the U.S.—they just don't know how and they're afraid to try." This only confirmed why it was so necessary for me to share what I had learned over the years.

I stayed in the home of a lovely Brazilian couple who didn't speak any English; however, their 13-year-old daughter was in the process of learning how. As I approached the house with bag in hand, the teenager greeted me. I smiled and asked, "Will you show me where I'm supposed to stay?"

"Go stay by yourself," she responded, with a much friendlier tone than her answer implied.

"I'm sorry," I said. "I was told that I was staying here," my confusion clearly visible.

Embarrassed, the young lady reacted as if knowing she had chosen the wrong words. She shook her head, then tried again. "I mean, how do you say? 'I'm glad you are here. Be comfortable.'"

I answered, "Make yourself at home!"

Together we laughed as the ice was broken.

This sweet girl interpreted for her family the entire time I was with them. Later, we saw one another in the states and laughed again at that first awkward moment where our mutual humility recognized our shared, imperfect humanity. A simple smile speaks a thousand languages, and a misplaced phrase overrides the fear of saying nothing at all.

As a result of staying in their home, I was overjoyed to hear that her father decided to go into full-time ministry.

England impressed me with its lush green countryside. In all of my travels, I had never seen a place that rivaled the beauty of American topography as the U.K. did. Sheep dotted the hills and meadows, and rivers meandered through lush valleys. The sea smelled of salty satisfaction as fisherman brought in their daily catch.

And in the midst of this jewel of an island, a spiritual coldness was as prevalent as the stiff thermals the birds glided upon. When teaching the *You Can Tell It!* seminar to church lay leaders in the West Midlands Region of England, if a crowd of twenty or thirty attended, that was considered to be a good day. Contrasted with the hundreds I had taught during some trips, it was a dismal showing for a metropolitan area of over two million people, second largest only to Greater London.

I was there for three days before moving on.

Edinburgh, Scotland, was a luxury in June with pleasant weather during this six-day trip. The teaching during the day paused only for a time of rest and study before the outreach began in the evening. I enjoyed visiting Haddington and Niddrie on another trip, the stunning scenery only adding to the flavor of the locals' thick brogue and lively personality.

One night, after preaching on the topic of salvation by grace through faith, a couple approached me to heartily disagree.

So I asked them, "Then what do you do with Ephesians 2:8-9?" as I turned to my Bible and read the verses aloud: "For by grace you have been saved through faith, and that not of yourselves; it is the gift of God, not of works, lest anyone should boast."

They replied irreverently, "That's what God thinks, not what we think."

Yes, it was a mockery, but one that evoked in me the very grace they were refusing to acknowledge. To respond to such an ungodly statement would have been pointless. My silent prayer instead was, *Father, forgive them, for they do not know what they do, and open their eyes to the Truth.*

North Wales was a four-day trip teaching evangelism for lay leaders of Baptist Ministries Worldwide. The Welsh landscape is known for its spectacular natural wonders, with pristine mountainous areas flourishing with waterfalls, lakes, and hiking trails; lowlands with velvety smooth fields and enormous boulders chaotically scattered on the ground to mystify small spectators gazing up at them.

I stayed in a guesthouse for visiting ministers, but sadly, my schedule was so full that I couldn't take in as much of the stunning scenery as I would have liked. But the Welsh locals were entertaining enough with their commonly spoken Celtic tongue, spirited music, and a warm welcome for international visitors passing through. They are widely known as one of the friendliest people, and my fond memories attest to that kindness.

Yugoslavia (now called Serbia and Montenegro), following the allied victory of World War II, consisted of six republics in a federation, with borders drawn along historical and ethnic lines. However, the breakup of the former Yugoslavia due to political upheavals in the early 1990s is confusing to outsiders. It can be just as difficult for its own inhabitants to explain it—Muslims, Serbs, and Croats each having their own view of its evolving society.

The Republic of Serbia, located in central and southeast Europe, is a place where religion has been a major factor in shaping the country's history and culture. Serbia is predominantly "professing" Christian with Orthodox Christians leading the way at 85%, Roman Catholic second at 6%, while Serbia's Protestant following is about 1% (50,000). Muslims comprise only 3% of the population, with Judaism being the smallest at approximately 575 people.

It's important to know just how devoted the people are to their faith, no matter which faith we're talking about. That said, I was there in 2002, sponsored by the pastor of a local church. This four-day visit was filled with unforgettable moments, one of which I would love to share with you.

At the end of a passionate week of teaching evangelism, I returned to the church on Sunday to preach a final message before heading back to Dallas. A local man was there and heard my message of salvation. Filled with the knowledge of Christ's love, forgiveness, and reconciliation, he went home to enjoy the afternoon. That very evening, he died.

I can't help but thank God that this dear man had words of truth echoing in his mind, bringing peace in his final hours—whether he knew them to be or not—with the assurance that Christ was waiting on the other side. As far as I know, he had already trusted Christ, which makes the story all the more sentimental to me. God knew that my sermon would be the last one that gentleman would ever hear. I take a deep breath and thank the Lord for the privilege of serving him.

Because of this poignant true story, I tell other preachers, "Always remember that there may be someone listening to you that is receiving their farewell sermon." I also remind them not to assume that those people listening know the sure way to heaven. That their words matter, and that the fundamental gospel must be shared.

When it comes to preaching the good news, do it with clarity, compassion, and conviction.

Canada, our "nice" neighbor to the north, has been a country I've delighted in many times over the years with a total of fifteen trips from 1975 to 2016. While Americans consider it a close cousin with a similar family history, I think it's a mistake to discount its own distinctly unique character.

One cannot understate the magnificence of Alberta. Though it shares the Rocky Mountains with the U.S., at its heart, it is a prairie province. But pockets of stunning canary-blue glacial lakes surrounded by dizzying peaks make for extravagant hiking and skiing.

Manitoba has a little bit of everything, with its dramatic Arctic tundra to the north, lakes and forests to the east, and grasslands to the west and south. It's yet another Canadian locale that makes me thank God that He invented nature. Its Aboriginal and Metís people have called it home for six thousand years and continue to enrich the culture today.

Ontario, "waterfall capital of the world," is by far the most populated province with more than thirteen million residents. It touts the spectacular Niagara Falls and more lakes than you can comprehend. Not to be outdone is the Toronto skyline with the easily recognized CN Tower piercing the sky at 1,800 feet. But my favorite fun fact about Ontario is that two-thirds of it is covered by forests.

New Brunswick is a Maritime province on the far eastern coast. Its Bay of Fundy, part of the Appalachian Mountain range, its scenic views of the Atlantic, and its collection of historical lighthouses can entice any visitor to lengthen their stay. The highlight for me, beyond sharing my faith, was eating fresh lobster and clams, and deeply breathing in the clean ocean air.

I've taught citywide *You Can Tell It!* seminars in Canada, spoken at outreaches, Operation Friendships, and Wild Game Feasts (we'll get to that later), and I have every intention of returning again. It's such a special part of me.

It's fair to say that everything that I've done in America, I've taken to Canada.

In all of my travels to various lands, the stunning array of cultures never ceased to inspire me. The western hemisphere, in comparison to other parts of the world, seems logistically closer to home, yet a world apart with its rich diversity, assorted languages, and levels of religious faith. My journeys have also taken me to the distant shores of Europe, Africa, and Asia, shared in the next chapter.

Is there a land too far to deliver the gospel message? None I can think of.

Twelve

Outreach to the Eastern Hemisphere

For our citizenship is in heaven, from which we also eagerly wait for the Savior, the Lord Jesus Christ.
Philippians 3:20

Over my lifespan, I've done some traveling. In the early days, I visited the West Indies, the Bahamas, U.S. Virgin Islands in the Caribbean, and also India and the Netherlands. Those journeys opened my eyes to the different cultures in the world and some stark realities that came with them. In Amsterdam, I went to the home and secret annex where Anne Frank, her family, and four others hid from German forces for two years during WWII.

I saw the window she gazed out of at a sliver of blue sky, praying for the day she could see it again in all of its expansive glory. I took in the simple photo of an innocent thirteen-year-old girl frozen in time. I noticed her height lovingly measured in pencil on the wall next to her sister's. And I was inspired by the unquenchable flame that fortified her to live in those dark days—until that flame was callously snuffed out.

In the Netherlands, I traveled to Holland to visit the "hiding place" in the ten Boom house where Corrie and her family hid Jews and resistance workers to escape detection from the Nazis. Looking inside that narrow closet just big enough for six adults to stand, I wondered how many souls had been sequestered within its tiny space. It gave me a sense of the anxiety and dread they lived with. The Germans never did find the hiding place on their own. Like the Frank family, they were betrayed by an informant.

No matter how much time passes, evil persists. But there is also that same Light shining, well able to extinguish the darkness, bringing hope to all who continue to look up into the heavens believing in a brighter tomorrow.

In the uncertain times we live, those are the hearts I hear calling to me from distant shores.

Dahmen, Germany, is a principality where the Word of Life Bible Institute brought me to teach. The school I stayed in, once a WWII communist headquarters, was converted into a Bible school. The irony was unavoidable—the same building devoted to war and killing was now used for teaching eternal life. I was there for a week and was able to get out and see some things that were hard to reconcile.

In February of 1944, Corrie ten Boom and her family were arrested by the German Secret Police. She was incarcerated in her hometown of Haarlem, Holland, and placed in solitary confinement for the next three months. After her last hearing in September, she and her sister,

Betsy, were deported to Germany. The women managed to stay together while at Ravensbruck concentration camp until Betsy's death in December of that same year.

I went to the camp for myself and sensed the fear and horror of intolerable abuses the Jews endured—thin clothing and bedding in freezing conditions, maggot infested food, grim sanitation, brutal work assignments, the violence, the torture, the manner of death, and the denigration done to their dead bodies.

Even decades after the war, the execution site and incinerator where the deceased victims were burned lay bare and open like an empty tomb. I saw the shallow holes dug in the ground where prisoners were buried alive—folded like paper, knees to the chins—and smothered to death.

It was all so ugly. Human beings exploited, experimented on, killed at the hands of their fellow man; the suffering muffled by the sound of pure hate. And I remembered why I was there ... to speak loud and clear enough for love to be heard.

Tóalmás, Hungary, is a village located in Pest (part of Budapest), which is on the east side of the Danube River. With a population of about 3,000, I stayed on the campus of the Word of Life Bible Institute.

The area looked like a storybook painting with its historical charm, picturesque castles and palaces. The fisherman's soup, stuffed cabbage leaves, meat pancakes, and goulash added to the trip's flavor. But it was the people and their kindness that I took away with me.

And just as quickly as it began, the two-day teaching trip was suddenly over.

The **Czech Republic** was another of the many countries in which I've been. Continuing to place an emphasis on training others, be they lay leaders, students, or pastors, they were ministers of the gospel gleaning evangelical tools from the *You Can Tell It!* or *You Can Preach It!* seminars.

It has always been my opinion that when you "preach," you will *add* to the kingdom. But when you "teach," you will *multiply* the effect—doubling, tripling, or quadrupling the end result. No one demonstrated this idea with more fluidity than Jesus who appealed to His apostles in the same way: to be "fishers of men."

Fish by yourself, and you will catch a fish. Teach others how to fish and together you will yield a boat full of fish. I've always felt the calling to multiply the catch.

Flanders, Belgium, was a town where I held a weeklong outreach and also taught. Though the economy was far better than many other countries where I had been—with jobs, shelter, and food security—it lacked an appetite for spiritual matters. The reason was a familiar one: a God of hope has little purpose for those who feel satisfied with the creature comforts they already possess.

It was my mission to open their eyes to see what they *did not* have—eternal life.

This duty to Christ came with a thoughtfully scheduled itinerary that permitted time for me to pray and study. It was a philosophy that has been a part of my life since the beginning. Studying the biblical text, researching its meaning, and praying for divine wisdom to understand it will only build up the body of Christ as I train others to do the same.

These short recesses allowed me to accomplish additional assignments God gave to me, such as writing the book, *Show Me How to Answer Tough Questions*, for Kregel Publications. The burden to start writing came after I heard Dr. James Dobson say, "Books can go where you can't and be hundreds of places at the same time." With a deadline looming, this particular summer trip was enhanced by the anticipation of the book's completion and release the following fall.

Moscow, Russia, opened up in late August 1991, two days after a failed coup attempt. Then newly elected president, Boris Yeltsin, suspended the Communist Party, and EvanTell was there to fill the void left by the appropriation of Christian freedom. After 70 years of communism, the Russian people were finally allowed to hear the gospel.

"According to some sources, the total number of Christian victims [persecuted] under the Soviet regime has been estimated to range around 12 to 20 million."[4] Along with the fall of communism came an economic crash, causing many people to lose their investments. Doctors were suddenly making $30 a month. All the years of hard work, reduced to nothing.

Most of the local homes were far too small to house guests, so the team from EvanTell along with members from Dallas area churches stayed in a hotel.

Our five-day evangelistic outreach was held at an old church in Moscow. Right away, I noticed that people

---

4 https://en.m.wikipedia.org/wiki/Persecution_of_Christians_in_the_Soviet_Union

struggled with a formidable barrier—the result of decades of social neglect. They believed that their sins were too great to be forgiven, and that God wouldn't accept them into His family or into heaven.

Their understanding of grace was as alien to them as the thought of their old communist government providing civil services. The concept of a free gift was completely foreign. It seemed so strange. In America, I had to convince folks that they *needed* to be saved. In Russia, I had to convince them that they *could* be saved. Their trust had eroded along with their faith in God.

And in this climate of emotional deterioration, it was explained to me that I should keep humor out of the message; that Russians didn't find it appropriate from the pulpit. However, when I got to know the locals, that statement was proved wrong. Parishioners loved humor in church, but it was the pastors who didn't think it was suitable.

Bucking the advice, I included little jokes (as I so often do) into the narrative, and the attendance grew every night after that. They laughed, felt uplifted and encouraged to trust in Christ. Also, the average age of the attendees went down, as the younger generation enjoyed the fresh environment that brought the freedom to speak your mind. To be entertained by a church service was novel, and they loved it.

By the end of the week, the local pastors asked if I would teach them how it was done. Me, the unlikely evangelist with a speech impediment, teach the art of humor in communication? *Go ahead and laugh.*

Apart from the outreach, we ventured out into the community (with an interpreter), door-to-door, to share the gospel. One to two hours on average was needed to bring a person to the Lord. It was difficult and slow going, but necessary. I knew that there were other believers coming to Russia who simply prayed a "prayer of decision" with a person, then moved on to the next, thinking that they had done their Christian duty—just another notch in their holy helmet of salvation, without doing the work. And that was inexcusable.

If a baby "Christian" lacks the understanding—the true knowledge of grace in Christ's sacrifice—the gesture of praying for salvation is useless. They have merely repeated words that have no meaning.

I recall a woman who told us that she had already become a Christian only weeks before. Making sure that it was true, I asked her where she was going if she died that night, and she replied, "To hell." She couldn't grasp what it meant to be saved. This lack of due diligence on the part of a few careless American missionaries was indefensible and lit a righteous anger in me.

Another conversation I had lasted a couple of hours with a particular woman, as she struggled to wrap her head around the core message of the gospel. Suddenly, at once, she threw up her hands and said, "I get it! You're telling me that it's a free gift! That's incredible!"

We truly enjoyed our time in Russia and all of the volunteers associated with the trip. To thank our amazing interpreter for doing such a great job, we treated her to lunch at the very first McDonald's to open in the country—a very big deal. It was over burgers and fries that I finally asked her the question she had repeated for me, time after time, when I presented it to others: "If you were to die tonight, do you know that you would go to heaven?"

She took a deep breath then smiled. "Every night, I've listened to you explain it," she said, "but now, I finally understand it." The light in her eyes told me that she did.

God used me to lead her to Christ right there. To think that while this McDonald's was being built, the owners, the financers, and even the interpreter (as she watched the structure slowly going up), never suspected that one day, God would choose that very place to lead people to Christ—to lead her to the Lord. Yes, God has plans for all of us, at the time and location of His choosing, including fast food joints.

Who are we to question where and when His miracles will occur?

Three years later in 1994, another team and I returned to Russia, this time to the town of Voronezh. Tammy accompanied me on every trip to Russia but wasn't able to sing due to the language barrier. Our son, David, was also with us on this trip, now a curious twelve-year-old.

In this foreign environment of unusual dialogue exchanges, there were questions posed to me that I had never heard in America. For instance, a man asked me, "If I'm on the train and someone steals my shirt, and he needs it more than I do, should I let him have it?" Then he continued, "If yes, how am I supposed to buy another shirt without any money?" I could only come to the painful conclusion that this bizarre fictional theft had actually happened to him.

Outreach to the Eastern Hemisphere

It's unconventional encounters like these—an "extravagant" lunch at McDonald's; a shirt stolen off of your back—that brings life into sharp focus. It made me realize that Russian people's tender hearts rested very close to the surface. I found them to be loving and empathetic.

Upon my return in 1995, 1996, and 1997, I felt the same connection to the citizens of Penza. They cried when we left. And we cried with them.

Siberia can conjure images of arid wilderness covered in ice and snow. With a radius of 1.5 million square miles, the Arctic Ocean lies to the north, and Kazakhstan lies to the south next to Mongolia and China. The 33 million inhabitants share a long and complex history. This explains the mixture of religions such as Buddhism, Islam, and the predominant faith of Orthodox Christian.

In April of 1999, the snow was starting to melt, and the countryside had lost its glacial sparkle. Its virgin white pack had been trampled on by the dirty boots of spring. Gone were the pillows of marshmallow-covered grasslands, leaving only muddy tracks and a disheveled appearance. But being a man who adores the outdoors, the sweet brisk air and tantalizing wildlife captured me. From the train window, I saw a moose!

Later, a gentleman I met who spoke English discovered that I loved to hunt and gave me an expensive book on the subject, which I still have. "I'll never be able to afford a hunting license again, so I want you to have this." The fee of $5 was an excessive amount in his post-communist life. As a fellow hunter, my heart broke for him.

I was there for six incredible days, teaching at the Krasnoyarsk Bible Institute. The men were pastors in training, and I was fortunate to be hosted by one of them (let's call him Sergey). His story is unique, and I think you'll be blessed if I share it with you.

Prior to coming to Christ, Sergey was involved with the wrong kind of people and ended up behind bars. While in jail, Sergey was so despised by a fellow inmate that the other prisoner took out a contract on his life, hiring a thug on the outside. But while waiting on Sergey's release, the hoodlum was arrested and jailed.

Training leaders in Siberia

In the interim, Sergey came to Christ before completing his jail time and release. Thirty miles away, in another prison, the hired killer was hearing the gospel message and also came to the Lord. The murder never happened.

Years later, a mission organization started a training school for men to become pastors, and a member thought that Sergey and his once would-be assassin would make extraordinary spiritual leaders. Unbeknownst to these two ex-cons who had never met before, they ended up sitting right next to each other in class.

Sergey cordially introduced himself to the former hired killer and asked him his name. As they shook hands, the man answered with stunned disbelief.

"I'm Ivan, and I was hired to kill you. But Jesus talked me out of it."

It's said that on earth, we reap what we sow; to live by the sword is to die by the sword; an eye for an eye and a tooth for a tooth. But the opposite occurs when Christ gets involved. Where evil plans to take life, Jesus steps in and saves it.

Kiev, Ukraine, has been enduring hostility from Russia for years due to the annexation of Crimea. And to see the images today coming out of that country under assault leads me to an ongoing prayer for their spiritual strength, political peace, and physical restoration. During my visit there in 2005 as a guest teacher at the Word of Life Bible Institute, I was privileged to train students, even leading several of them to Jesus while they prepared for ministry.

That was true nearly everywhere I went on foreign soil. I was introducing "Christians" to Christ for the first time. So many of them weren't truly saved in the proper context of Christianity for lack of understanding the gospel of grace. That trusting in Jesus alone could save you. But now many of them were.

The Unlikely Evangelist

South Korea is a free society sharing a border with one of the most isolated and unsympathetic dictatorships on the planet. We made trips to Seoul in 1995, 1996, 1997, and 1999, and every time, I was deeply aware of the tension below the surface—an underlying fear of what could happen if North Korea decided to flex its military muscle. Still, life went on. The threat, largely ignored.

The city of Seoul was progressive, a combination of a high-tech age and an old-world humility. We stayed in a lovely hotel in the heart of the city, and the people I met were warm and hospitable. Like many Asian countries, politeness is ingrained into the culture; to respect and honor others.

Preaching through an interpreter in Korea

My hosts opened the door for me, refused to let me carry my own briefcase, and lavished me with kindness and support. Ultra-accommodating, they asked what kind of food my favorite was, then took me to the finest restaurants that served my taste. I ate some of the most delicious cuisine I would ever have while traveling.

I was equipped with an expert interpreter—an absolute necessity for speaking at one of the largest churches in Seoul, teeming with thousands of parishioners rivaling any megachurch in the states. The electricity of the Spirit lit the room and can only be described as holy intoxication. To be used in such a way, for the benefit of so many halfway around the world, brought me to my knees.

Each trip to South Korea only added to my catalog of treasured memories and hopes of returning, to practice the principle of multiplication by equipping others in evangelism.

The Republic of the Philippines is nestled in Southern Asia, with 109 million[5] polite, fun-loving, and spiritually receptive people. Over 7,500 islands sprinkle the area in the western Pacific Ocean, which provide an infinite number of beaches to stroll on while appreciating kaleidoscope sunsets at the end of the day.

To my delight, I discovered that Filipinos not only have an amazing sense of humor but can laugh at themselves just as quickly. And since English is widely spoken, I had little trouble translating puns.

The art of propriety begins at a tender age and is built into the fabric of their culture. Gracious behavior comes naturally to their friendly demeanor, with "sir" and "ma'am" used to address foreigners, no matter what age they might be. They also call an older man "kuya" (big brother) and woman "ate" (big sister), despite the lack of

---

5 https://en.wikipedia.org/wiki/Philippines

blood relation. The elderly, disabled, and even pregnant women queue up in a special line at banks in order to make their lives easier.

Equipping pastors in the Philippines

If the locals love anything as much as they do socializing, it's eating—breakfast, lunch, and dinner with a "merienda," a term used for *snack or dessert,* enjoyed in between. Rice with every meal is common and usually served with fish, soaking up tasty broths, assorted vegetables and fresh fruit. Most protein in the Filipino diet comes from eggs, seafood, chicken, and dairy, all placed before you with welcoming congeniality.

Outreach to the Eastern Hemisphere

I flew into the capital city of Manila in February of 2014, at the invitation of the Word of Life Bible Institute. The three-day conference was held in a building open to anyone who had an interest in learning how to evangelize. Roughly 125 attendants came, consisting of pastors, teachers, and Christian devotees.

I would travel to the Philippines twice, and both times I felt the hand of God moving mightily.

Uganda, Africa, in 2001, was a country in which a local church was building a new facility and was looking for ways to induce people to come. I was invited and stayed at the house of the pastor during our six-day outreach. Never before had I met a man of faith whose salary was paid in goats, milk, and crops. It gave me an additional layer of gratitude for my own country and personal circumstances.

Uganda is an arid landscape experiencing biannual rainy seasons in the spring and fall, making the soil as murky as its former notorious military dictator, Idi Amin. Though he was ousted from power in 1979, the effects remain in the psyche of Ugandans. The country's economy was devastated by his policies, and it still struggles financially despite its decreased poverty rate over time.

One day, as I was teaching to about twenty locals in a scruffy canvas tent, they asked me to stop.

"Please, let us go and get the people in the next village. They'll want to hear this, too!"

When I agreed, some of them scurried off, then returned with thirty more folks. These precious people would become the new church. In fact, before the building was even completed, the church had a full congregation.

I later returned to Africa and taught in Tanzania. Afterward, several of my students, consisting of pastors and church leaders, shared that they had never before understood the gospel—until God used me to explain it.

It was plain that I wasn't always training people who knew the Lord, though most of them believed that they did. However, hearing the lectures, they realized that it wasn't true. Teaching, speaking, and ministering in foreign countries, I've strived to educate those who should, by all accounts, give a better sermon than myself as they communicate to fellow countryman in their own native tongue. I hope and pray that my efforts have not been in vain.

My travels have spanned decades and include visits to a variety of cities, villages, and communities in the countries I've mentioned—a total of over 60 foreign locations. Domestically speaking, by the time this book is released in 2023, I will have taught and evangelized in all fifty states—God willing.

One of the most gratifying things I've enjoyed in my journeys to distant shores is the development of lifelong relationships. Pastors continue to invite me to their churches, and even their children who are now pastors of their own churches invite me as well. I've always seen myself as a servant to the worldwide church, and I've served some of the finest pastors I've ever known—some still on earth, some now in heaven.

Heaven—our final destination. Though my calling in this life is to minister to citizens of this world, I look forward to the day when I am reunited with family and friends in God's kingdom. There are so many souls that wait for me in the life to come. Dear ones I have loved and missed in their absence. Those relationships are never far from my mind, and their influence is always with me.

Thirteen

Ray of Sunshine

But there is a friend who sticks closer than a brother.
Proverbs 18:24b

Colorado has a rugged, romantic quality about it. The desert lands, dusty canyons and colorful mesas are reminiscent of the old west, unchanged for centuries. The Colorado Rockies boast the tallest peaks in the 3,000-mile chain that runs from Southern New Mexico up to northern British Columbia.

Modern-day explorers thirsty for untamed wildness come from all over to enjoy some of the finest hunting grounds in the lower forty-eight. It was on a hunt with a new friend, Ray Jones, that I came to respect the precarious nature of those magnetic mountains and all the dangers hidden there.

Hailing from Raymond, Mississippi, not far from his church in Jackson, Ray had heard my associate, Cam Abell, teach the *You Can Tell It!* seminar in 1995. It made an indelible impression. So much, that when I went there to speak at an evangelism conference the following year, Ray was eager to attend.

When I concluded my message, the pastor invited me to dinner. And discovering that I was an avid hunter, Ray tagged along. I found him to be humble, gentle-spirited, and we hit it off immediately. As we broke bread and shared life experiences, Ray and I quickly bonded over our love of evangelism and hunting.

Every now and then, we find ourselves in the company of a long-lost friend that we have never met before. Yet, after only a few minutes in their presence—listening to their ideas, sensing their passions for like-minded pursuits—we know that they will always be a part of our life going forward. That's how I felt about Ray. In him, I found a kindred companion. He understood the true essence of grace as I did, and we would go on to discuss the subject for hours at a time.

Our first hunting trip together was in the imposing atmosphere of the Colorado mountains.

Selfless

It was a pleasant day with moderate temperatures as we hiked up the mountain to our midway camp along with another hunter. The strong smell of pines was a powerful tonic as my mind acclimated from the commotion of civilization to the soundproofed soil of a silent forest. We reached base camp late morning and dropped off our gear. Then, Ray and I set out for an afternoon of hunting on the mountainside.

Ray of Sunshine

Every seasoned hunter knows to stay with their "buddy" while tracking big game. And we did—at first. But as our pace shifted from lockstep to individual strides, the space that separated us grew wider. Perhaps the two-way radios we carried lulled us into a misconceived safety as we focused on the trail just under our own feet. Before long, we drifted far apart.

As the sun sank and the treetops disappeared into darkness, my radio suddenly crackled with a familiar voice that should have been close by, but wasn't.

"Larry, I can't seem to figure out where I am," Ray's concern scratched through the receiver. "I think I'm lost."

His troubling words sent a chill through the fading warmth of that late October evening as it abruptly turned cold. The temperature was comfortable when we started out that afternoon. Ray's lightweight T-shirt was enough to filter out the crisp air as we canvased the autumn landscape for elk. Now, the breeze had a bite as the sun dipped below the horizon. Night had come upon us and brought with it below freezing conditions. In a matter of hours, exposed to the elements, Ray could suffer hypothermia and his body could shut down.

Then ... *it began to rain.*

I headed back to camp and informed Darwin, the other hunter who was with us, that Ray was missing. We optimistically reassured one another that he would appear at any minute. All night, I prayed for Ray to find his way back as the bad weather persisted.

By morning, Ray still hadn't made it in, and I was sick at the thought that he may not come back at all. Dreading the worst, Darwin and hiked to the bottom of the mountain to notify Search and Rescue. The Forest Service and volunteers were organized and dispatched to begin an all-out hunt for Ray. *How could we have let this happen?*

What would I say to his wife and their son with special needs? "I'm sorry, Diane, but your husband died last night on a frozen mountaintop." The words ricocheted around my brain, and I was terrified I would have to eventually speak them out loud. I prayed and prayed that God would demonstrate His trademark grace and mercy—the same grace that Ray and I were so confident of.

Then, like a heavenly balm that covered me with peace, God's words of promise replaced my own troubled thoughts: "Be anxious for nothing, but in everything by prayer and supplication, with thanksgiving, let your requests be known to God; and the peace of God, which surpasses all understanding, will guard your hearts and minds through Christ Jesus" (Philippians 4:6-7). I clung to His words like the moss that hugged the soggy bark of wooden centurions holding up the drizzling sky.

Finally, there was a message from the game warden that Ray had been found by another hunter—eight miles off course. He was alive. When they brought him into camp, soaking wet, stiff and shivering, we embraced each other with sobs. Other hunters aware of the circumstances said that they didn't know how he managed to survive the night. That it was *humanly* impossible.

But it was a trilogy of wisdom Ray packed with him that made all the difference: he kept moving; he headed downhill, and he didn't panic.

Ray's constant motion all through the night, though exhausting, kept him warm in the frigid hours between dusk and dawn. Had he stopped to rest, exposure would have taken him. Ray continued to move down the mountain, knowing that with lower elevation comes warmer temperatures and more people. And finally, anxiety was stifled by his faith that kept him from panicking.

"For some reason, I wasn't at all afraid," Ray confided. "I never worried about a thing. I knew God was with me, and that He would save me."

This first hunting trip together forged a concrete connection between us that would last a lifetime.

A sidebar to this story is worth mentioning. It illustrates Ray's sweet nature and sensitivity toward others, even strangers. About 3:00 o'clock in the morning, as he wandered in the dark—freezing and vulnerable—Ray came upon a hunter's trailer. But not wanting to bother the folks asleep inside, he kept going thinking he would eventually find his way to camp.

"You could have lost your life," I told him, "and caused a lot of people terrible grief just because you didn't want to interrupt someone's sleep."

"You're right," he said. "But I just couldn't trouble them."

As we packed up to leave camp, he continued to apologize for ruining our hunt. But that was so like him. Whether it was the time he dedicated, the energy he spent, or the money he provided (blessed with financial freedom), Ray gave and gave, then gave some more. Mostly, he gave away pieces of his heart. But it was big enough for everyone he met.

The Unlikely Evangelist

*My favorite picture of Ray Jones from
one of our many hunting trips*

Humans have a great capacity to love if they are so inclined. Sadly, there are a lot of folks who choose to love themselves above all else. But Ray was a case study in sunshine. His love flowed out from him in every direction, undiscriminating, revealing the goodness that we all are capable of. Even behind black clouds, his light was never far from breaking through if you were fortunate enough to be standing near him.

Love Has No Bounds

As men, it can be difficult (even impossible) for us to admit that we love another man. Call it pride, fear of appearing effeminate, or bringing into question our sexuality. But there are still a few of us who believe that a proper love is a right and a reward when we open our hearts to everyone—even those of our own gender. Worry of condemnation is a sad reason to keep love from those we feel connected to, like a dear friend. I have found that to reflect Christ in His truest form is to love unconditionally, and to express that love in words, action, and sacrifice.

But as adults, how often do we say the words, "You're my best friend," out loud for someone to hear? Ray was fearless in that way and said those words to me as easily as any others. And I would say them in return. Just speaking affirmation to someone can place a cushion of care around them that they may not find anywhere else. As a child of God, it's our place in this world to shine His love without reservations.

There is nothing to be ashamed of when Jesus is at the center of your love.

It was this kind of transparency that also enabled Ray and me to share loving rebukes that only best friends can say without causing offense. And the words, "I'm sorry" also came effortlessly to us when confronted with a painful truth. Integrity, humility, and generosity were the character traits that guided and guarded us in our long and loving friendship. There was never a moment of tension between us. We could relax. To be present in the moment is an art that I wish more people practiced.

Like me, Ray had a heart for the lost. When he discovered that I regularly went on foreign mission trips, he asked if he could come along. Of course, it gave me great joy to have him. In Russia, he was with me on our door-to-door visits. He helped me minister to locals of all ethnicities and religious backgrounds in India and Africa.

Wherever we went, Ray was constantly talking about the Lord—to flight attendants, the person sitting next to him, game wardens, hunting guides, hotel owners, strangers on the street—everyone and anyone who would listen. I can tell you without hesitation that no one else used EvanTell's Bad News/Good News tract more than Ray.

I describe our connection as a "David and Jonathan relationship" like the shepherd David and Jonathan, the eldest son of King Saul. Their loyalty to each other (found in 1 Samuel, chapters 19 and 20) reveals the devotion Ray and I had for one another. We would have died for each other, and I don't say that casually. I mean it literally. "Greater love has no one than this, than to lay down one's life for his friends" (John 15:13).

We told each other what we *needed* to hear, not always what we *wanted* to hear. I relied on his gentle brand of truth whether it was easy to listen to or not. Once, on an elk hunting trip, we weren't in the truck for very long when he said to me, "Larry, I know you came for the hunt. But I came to talk about you. I think you need to slow down and take more breaks, so you have a longer life."

Those words would turn out to be a precursor to a health event that could have shortened my life dramatically. We'll talk about that later. But for now, let's concentrate on Ray.

The Reason Why We're Here

What red-blooded hunter doesn't fantasize about going on an African safari? It was always something I had hoped to do, but they are extremely expensive. So, when a friend called me one day and asked if I'd like to go, I answered, "No thanks. I'm a minister, not a millionaire."

But in 2009, when the American economy tanked, African ranchers made adjustments to lure visitors over. Instead of holding to the usual safari cost of thousands of dollars, they were now offering them for hundreds. This same friend told me about a rancher with inexpensive hunting packages that I could afford. Starry-eyed at the prospect, I ended up joining him and his buddy on a guided hunt. And since all hunters are required to go out in pairs, Ray came with me. Honestly, he was the only one I wanted to ask on this week-long adventure.

Namibia, located in southern Africa, with its diverse wildlife (including a cheetah population) held all of my long-lived expectations for this dream-come-true. Ray and I got to room together. We started each morning with prayer and devotions, and with our Colorado calamity still fresh in our minds, this time Ray and I stuck together like pitch on a maple tree.

With a local guide, we were taken to the best locations to spot wild game. Hunting etiquette dictates that each person takes a turn—with a single shot—when an animal is in range. If that hunter misses, it is customary for his buddy to take the next shot. On the first day, I took down a species of antelope called a Kudu. I was like a kid again, back in Pennsylvania, elated with the prize I had wanted so badly.

Now it was Ray's turn. He was a good hunter and a good shot. Unfortunately, quick shots were not his strength, and the majority of African shooting requires a fast spot, aim, and fire. The animals are simply too fast on their feet to do it any other way.

Poor Ray, the sweetest guy in the world, kept missing. And I felt for him.

Sometimes, we would nest in a hunting blind set up to offer a concealed place with better vantage points. Ray, being uncommonly generous, would always insist that I take it. He refused to have it for himself.

One night, after a long but exciting day out in the bush, I sat on the edge of the bed thinking about where I was, the amazing company I was with, and a thought impressed me: *When I see the Lord, He's not going to ask me, "What did you shoot in Africa, Larry?" but "How did you treat Ray?"* It was a spiritual epiphany that came with a twinge of guilt.

This was a trip of a lifetime, and I wanted to get a lot of animals. I had envisioned it so many times. But day after day, Ray kept missing his quarry. Finally, I came to terms with what this trip was really about—the real reason why I was there.

"Lord, I don't care if I go home without the animals I came for. I'm not going take another shot until Ray scores an animal."

Convicted and committed to this, I told Ray what I promised the Lord. He responded in the same selfless way I had grown accustomed to.

"You don't have to do that, Larry. I wouldn't be here if it weren't for you, and I really want you to have a great time."

But as I held to that promise, Ray began to hit his target. More than once! But the Kudu he hit took off running, and we couldn't find it until the next day. We spread out to search for it, and when I found it, his excitement exploded. "You found it, Larry!" he yelled from 100 yards away. "My best friend found my Kudu!" *David and Jonathan*, always and forever.

By the time we returned home to the states, we had enjoyed an incredibly successful hunt and made memories that would be difficult to top.

It's ventures like these that make me wish they could go on forever. Then something unexpected happens—unforeseen and terrible—that reminds me that we live in a fallen world, and the fragile flesh we wear only lasts a short while.

Still Shining

In 2015, Ray was being bothered by some physical symptoms he couldn't explain. Noticing slight rigidity in his body and a tremor in his hand, he sought a medical opinion to put his mind at ease. Surely, it was the natural process of getting older and that was all.

When the diagnosis came back as Parkinson's Disease, he knew that things would only get worse—taking his freedom, his bodily functions, and finally his life. The news was devastating to all of us. The thought that my dearest friend would lose control of his limbs and lungs and would eventually shake uncontrollably, was more than I could stand.

Depending on the severity of the disease, doctors say that life expectancy can be anywhere from ten to twenty years. However, in some cases, it is less than seven.

The sadness that comes with a diagnosis of this magnitude sinks into your bones. We all felt it. To bid your body goodbye while still residing in it is a cruel eviction. I knew that eventually Ray's speech would be gone, and we would no longer have our special talks about the Lord. But this shocking illness only tied us in an even greater love and understanding of relationship—for each other and for others.

Four years later, Ray struggled but held on with the loving support of his wife, Diane. Then she died unexpectedly of a brain aneurysm. This left Ray alone, again, out on a mountainside, weak and leaning on God's saving grace. At the front of his mind was how he would care for his special needs son, Kevin, who was now a 48-year-old. I can't begin to know what that must have been like for him. To lose the love of his life so swiftly, assuming that she would survive him, and now he was the sole stability for his only child.

I'm convinced that suffering in the body has a spiritual value that none of us are able to see until viewed from above. Like a grand tapestry with each thread thoughtfully woven into place, how painful are the tangles we endure on this side. But the knots that secure us must enhance its beauty—if only to glorify the Weaver and His extravagant work.

We may be thrown down, and lie helpless beneath the feet of tragedy, but Christ has walked this path already. He has traveled miles, been beaten to the ground, and hung high for all to see. But His design is perfect. His life is everlasting. And we must obediently follow Him.

In 2020, I was in Mississippi driving Ray and myself to hunt deer. He sat next to me as we approached the decided place. Then Ray's phone began to ring. It was Kevin's caretaker, Pam.

"Please have Larry bring you home. Kevin is unresponsive."

Knowing what this meant, we turned the truck around in a rainstorm that had suddenly unleashed a torrent of tears. It was the longest hour we had ever spent together, suspended in a downpour that kept us at a steady but tedious twenty-five mph. Halfway home, Ray checked in with Pam to see how Kevin was doing.

She hesitated, then asked, "Ray, are you behind the wheel?"

"No, Larry is driving," steeling himself for what she would say next.

"Kevin has passed away."

Ray left his son, unaware it would be the last time he would see him alive. I was overwhelmed that God would bring me to Mississippi, so that I would be with him when he received the news that his boy had died. Crying harder than I've ever seen any man cry, Ray poured out his love in wails. Another piece of his heart, gone. When we finally arrived at the house, close friends were already congregating there. Ray entered, leaned over Kevin's lifeless body, and wept.

His sorrow was visceral, and was magnified by his own illness and the empathy in the room. Within one year, Ray's soulmate and their child had been taken. After that, his physical condition got weaker resulting in multiple falls that discouraged his spirit but never to the detriment of others. Incredibly, Ray's light continued to shine.

Ray's wife, Diane, and their special needs son, Kevin

The next year, I made a point of getting back to Mississippi to hunt with Ray again. But his strength had deteriorated, making it difficult for him to move around though he insisted on doing so. Nothing brought him more joy, other than the Lord, than for us to go out hunting together. It would be the last time.

At Day's End

Over the course of twenty-six years, Ray and I trekked some pretty remarkable territory, hunting together in Canada, Africa, New Mexico, Colorado, Louisiana, Mississippi, Nebraska, and Texas. It seemed that God was chuckling when He introduced us to each other. He knew that the Bible and big game would connect us and seal our spirits into a single unit of faith and friendship.

Toward the end of Ray's sickness, he asked me to come to Mississippi to hunt wild turkey. In 2022, the April spring had sprung and hunting fever was upon us. But considering his obvious decline, I couldn't find it in me to put him through it.

"Ray, I hate to say it, but there's no way you can go hunting anymore," I said with uncensored yet necessary openness. "But I've got a better idea," I continued. "Why don't I come down there on Memorial Day weekend, and we'll just sit and talk?"

"You're right. Come on over," he said after digesting the uncomfortable honesty.

This time, Tammy was with me as I drove the six hours from Dallas to Ray's home. Not so coincidentally, his love for me was also transferred to her, and the mutual affection ran deep. It was Friday when we arrived to find him in his bedroom nestled in a hospital bed. He had 24-hour care due to his failing health, and now his speech was severely compromised. But it didn't keep him from smiling.

There are things God leaves with some of us that are just too precious to take away. For Ray, laughter was one of them.

After a little while, Tammy left the room so we could have some private time. As I sat next to him, thinking of the evening we met over dinner so long ago, I realized how much he had invested in my life. The little idiosyncrasies that made our polar opposite personalities even funnier together. He was always getting too cold, and I was always overheating. I walked fast and he walked slowly. I was organized and prepared while Ray was less than methodical. But we found beauty in our differences and learned to love what set us apart. That folks are more than just outward appearance but made of the same stuff inside. The same earth and stardust and sunshine—the things that best described him.

Ray and I talked, and I thanked him for everything: for what he meant to me and how my life was made richer with him being in it. I read scripture to him, and we prayed. And when I walked out for the last time the following Monday, the final words he would ever say to me were, "Thank you, Larry."

I answered in the only way I knew how. "I love you Ray."

There was no guarantee I would see him again, this side of the Tapestry. After that trip, Ray's light began to fade. I could sense it in the spirit and steadied myself for the coming inevitable.

Eight days later, Ray went to be with the Lord.

Years earlier on a hunting trip, Ray asked me a question that required a promise. "If I go before you, Larry, will you give my memorial message?" It was a promise I would now make good on.

Three days after his death, back in Mississippi, I spoke at the service about someone that had departed but left an enormous amount of love behind him. The message came from Psalm 23 with the theme, *The Lord is my shepherd, and that's enough.* That was the narrative of Ray's life.

Back at home in Dallas, in tears I took the rifle, scope and sling that Ray had given me several years before, and held them close. In his absence, joy overflowed as I pictured him—Ray had reached the mountaintop. He wasn't lost. He wasn't cold or alone.

He was shining.

Fourteen

Stories from the Field

"No one can come to Me unless the Father who sent Me draws him; and I will raise him up at the last day."
John 6:44

I love stories. Especially if they have a redeeming quality that teaches me something or inspires me to be a better person. A comedy can lift the heart and a romance can send it soaring just as easily as a tragedy can break it. Stories can cultivate empathy and kindness, courage and caution. Most of all, they can stir emotions and challenge us to change.

My favorite narratives are those based in fact; ones that I personally identify with. The characters have an authenticity that brings back memories of people I've known—for good or for bad. The following stories are only a fraction of the events that I've seen and heard in my years of ministry. Keep in mind that many of the names have been changed to protect privacy, but all of the incidents did happen.

I hope they will inspire you to look deeper into all of God's workings, and that you allow Him to write a new story in your life every day.

The Lame Will Walk, the Blind Will See

Ken suffered from diabetes. He was missing a leg and wore the internal scars of psychological damage. He had carried a heavy burden since childhood, growing up with an abusive father. When I said hello to him, he wept tenderly, overcome by emotion.

"That story changed my life. That story changed my life," he kept repeating.

I was in Houston, Texas, the guest of Sunday school teacher, Chuck Cummings, instructing a mini seminar called *How to Respond to Those Who Say They Are Christians and Act Like They're Not*. That day, Chuck had invited his non-Christian brother-in-law, Ken, who was nearly sixty years old. After the class, Chuck approached me to say that Ken wanted to speak with me. He then led me to a man in a wheelchair who was crying.

The story I shared that Ken was so touched by was an experience that happened years earlier as I was presenting the gospel to a gentleman. It went like this:

"Wait a minute, don't go any further!" the man abruptly stopped me. "I know everything you're going to tell me. That eternal life is a free gift because Christ died on a cross for my sins, and if I put my trust in Him, He'll save me."

"Yes, that's exactly right," I smiled.

"Look, I believe all that is true. But I don't want to trust Christ."

I asked him why and he replied, "Because I genuinely believe that my dad understood what it was to be a Christian, and that he was a Christian. There is no question in my mind that he is now in heaven. But if he's in heaven, I want to go to hell."

"Why would you want that?" I asked, disturbed by his sincerity.

He explained that no one else had ever seen the terrible way his father treated his mother and the family. Although he appeared to be a great Christian out in the world, he was a horrible Christian inside the home. Then Ken repeated the sentiment again, "If he's in heaven, hell is fine with me."

"You know what I find amazing? Your dad controlled you all through life, and now you're saying he gets to control your eternity, too. In other words, your time on earth was often a living hell. But now, you're going to allow him to put you through hell forever."

The man shook his head and admitted that he had never thought about it that way. It gave him pause, and perhaps a reason to reconsider.

That was the illustration in my message that affected Ken so deeply: that regardless of how Christians may disappoint us, we cannot let them keep us from trusting Jesus.

It's true that people often transfer their feelings about their earthly father onto their heavenly one. And Ken's tears were evidence of that. But now, he recognized it—that the memory of his hypocritical dad was keeping him from the compassion of Christ. On that Sunday, Ken trusted Christ as his Savior.

About a year later, Chuck called to tell me that Ken was so enthusiastic to be a Christian that he had been baptized! In front of the entire congregation—from wheelchair to water—he was carried into the pool by three fellow Christians, making a public declaration of his faith.

As in many churches, it's customary for the friends and family to clap as they celebrate for the person coming out of the water. On this occasion, the entire church body stood to their feet and applauded with tears and cheers. Ken is now with the Lord, but wherever he went, he told the story of how everything changed the day he laid aside his past prejudices and trusted Christ.

Ken couldn't walk, so others carried him. He couldn't see further than the pain of his past, but the grace of God opened his eyes to the truth. He was broken in mind and body, but a simple story offered him a new life. And he took it.

You're Not What I Expected!

"I have to confess," a woman said to me after I had just finished giving a special lecture on evangelism in the Atlanta area. "You really surprised me—in a good way."

"In what way?" I asked.

"When they told me you were an evangelist, that you had gone to Bible college and were even a professor, I thought, *Oh, no, here we go again!* He's going to put us on a guilt trip for not evangelizing and tell us how ashamed we ought to be that we don't talk more to others about Christ." She grinned and continued, "But I was pleasantly surprised. You were everything *but* that. And I have to admit, after listening to you, I came away really wanting to talk to others about Jesus."

She seemed so pleased, but I was saddened that what she said was true and epitomized what people expect from evangelists. They have earned a reputation of using guilt to motivate others to evangelize.

I pray that more and more evangelists are *not* what people expect.

Six Short Days

Even in the month of February, Sun City, Arizona, is a beautiful place to have a Friendship Dinner. While there, I stayed with a delightful couple, Les and Lydia, a gem of a pair. As I deplaned and descended the steps of the airport, Les literally ran over and hugged me.

"Larry, it's so good to see you. I'm so glad you're here!" Never had I been received so sweetly by a total stranger.

Overtaken with his genuine warmth, I fought back tears as we embraced. He was a person who exuded nothing but kindness, goodness, and grace. So, on the way to the dinner, he said something that surprised me a little.

"Larry, I really feel discouraged. I'm trying to reach people of my own age (early sixties), but they're so set in their ways. I just can't seem to persuade them to trust Christ." His heart was nearly breaking as his dearest prayer remained unanswered.

When I returned home to Dallas, satisfied with the dinner that had been such a success, my spirit still ached for Les and his words that stayed with me: *I'm so discouraged.*

One week later, I received word that Les had gone to be with the Lord. I called his wife, Lydia, and we cried as she shared that he had suffered a massive heart attack—the heart that was so troubled was now at peace. I was comforted to know that he was in the presence of the Lord. But more than that, Lydia revealed the events of his life in those final six days.

After our time together, Les was so reenergized about evangelism that he read three of my books in two days, and even left several pages of handwritten notes in the copy of *Show Me How to Answer Tough Questions*. While at the golf course, he struck up a conversation with a fellow golfer who was going through some difficult times. Then Les turned the topic to faith.

"Has anyone ever taken a Bible and showed you how you can know for sure that you can go to heaven?" he asked him.

When this person told him no, Les took the time to explain the grace of Christ in detail. Several moments later, he led the man to Christ. Les, being only a few years old in the Lord himself, was so elated, he phoned Lydia right away.

"You won't believe what just happened! I led a man to the Lord!"

Listening to Lydia, a joy swelled up in me at the thought of Les seeing Jesus, face to face, only one day after introducing someone to Him.

The Thirty-Year Prayer

It was in Sequim, Washington, where a man in his late sixties and his wife approached me after I had given a message at a local church.

"I need to thank you for being instrumental in my salvation," he said, as he extended his hand and shook mine. "Eighteen years ago, you spoke at a church in Painesville, Ohio. It was a weeklong outreach, and I came every night. Many members of the church were praying for me."

He had my full attention as he continued. "They had such a burden for me, that you and Pastor Kirk stopped by my house to talk more with me as you were en route to the airport. As you may or may not remember, I was still resisting. But what you never knew was that right after you left, I trusted Christ—before you even made it to your gate."

Later, I came to discover that there were people who had been praying for him for thirty years prior to our conversation. He and his wife began to faithfully attend Sequim Bible Church, and their son is now in full-time Christian service.

Priority #1

To say that Chuck was in a financial bind would be putting it mildly. It was Friday evening when he got a call from his banker about his outstanding loan. This was serious.

The week before, a friend of Chuck's invited him to attend a meeting at his church. He politely refused, citing other commitments. Turns out, the "meeting" was one of my weeklong outreaches, happening Sunday through Friday. Each night, he got another invitation, and each time, he declined.

By Wednesday evening, his friend said, "Look, Chuck, you keep coming up with excuses. Friday is the last night, and I want your *word* that you'll come. I know your word is your bond."

Friday, before the service, Chuck got a reminder call about his promise to attend that last evening. He was still at his business sixty miles away, and he told his friend that he'd do his best to be there. At 5:00 pm, he received the phone call from his banker who said he needed to meet with him immediately. However, Chuck reluctantly told him that he had a prior engagement.

"What's more important than an outstanding $300,000 loan? The federal auditors will be here tomorrow!"

Obviously, Chuck couldn't tell him he was on his way to church just because he had given his word. But he stuck to his guns and headed to the church service. Halfway there, he convinced himself that he was crazy, and he turned the car around to meet with his banker.

"Wait a minute. I can't break my word. It's all I have."

Again, he turned back for church. A half-mile later, "I am crazy! I have to face the Feds tomorrow, and I'm going to a church service?" He turned the wheel and, suddenly, he was headed back to the office.

"What am I doing? My word is the most important thing I have. When I give it, it's always good. My whole life, my values, are based on what I consider to be my best asset."

Once again, the car pivoted in the opposite direction, and he arrived at the church just in time to slip into a seat beside his wife and his friend.

As I was introduced and greeted everyone, my unmistakable speech pattern befuddled Chuck. He glanced at his wife with a look of contempt. Her silent stare back at him amounted to *'Shut up and listen!'*

That final evening, my message was about trust: trusting an airline pilot to fly you in safety; trusting a chair to keep you from falling; trusting those things that can be seen and felt. Then I ended on a topic less physically tangible, but all the more important – trusting Christ as your only way to heaven.

"While all eyes are closed (and be honest with yourself right now), if you died tonight, are you certain you would go to heaven?"

Chuck realized that he just didn't know. There wasn't much he could trust in. Life was precarious, money was transient, and there was no guarantee what would happen from day to day. He wasn't an atheist, but he was uncertain. He had been counting on his good works and "word of honor" to earn his way into heaven—if there was such a place. Now, he was confronted with the uncomfortable truth that his eternal future was one big question mark, along with everything else that he was dealing with.

Following the service, Chuck met with me privately. After banter and debate, I was unable to convince him that trusting in Christ was the smartest, safest thing he could ever do. Then I asked him if I could pray for him.

He agreed, thinking it would conclude the philosophical discussion with me so he could leave.

But as I prayed, something incredible happened to him, and he interrupted me midway through. He told God—in his own words—that he was trusting Christ as his only way to heaven.

Chuck was grateful for the determination of his friend not to take "no" for an answer. He was also thankful for the ministry of EvanTell. If not for that night, he felt he may have never trusted Christ as his Savior.

The world and its fixtures—work, ambition, money, control—have little value in God's economy. The only thing we truly have is our word and *His*.

Take Nothing for Granted

Operation Friendship has been such a blessing to so many folks over the years. In Bradenton, Florida, I was speaking at just such a dinner. The host associate pastor and his wife invited their non-Christian neighbor couple to attend. They, in turn, asked if they could bring a couple. The associate pastor knew who they were speaking of and assumed that they were believers due to prior conversations with them where they talked about their church and faith.

When the dinner was concluding and the invitation to trust Christ was given, not only did the unbelieving man and his wife respond to Christ, but so did the couple assumed to be Christian. That gentleman came up to me afterward.

"Larry, if Jesus Christ had asked me why I should be let into heaven, I would *not* have said, 'Because You died for me.' I've never understood the meaning of His death—until now."

This example is often repeated as I have moved through "Christian" circles. I've discovered that the identities of some people are not as they appear. It has taught me a valuable lesson: never assume a "Christian" is saved. Take *nothing* for granted.

Never Heard of Him

While at the Word of Life Bible Institute in Kiev, Ukraine, I participated in a street meeting with some of the students. Cleverly, they would use a drawing board to attract people passing by, then strike up a conversation with those who were interested in talking about Christ. It was there that I met two men from Iran, who had arrived six months earlier. Fortunately, they spoke English.

They told me they had never heard of Jesus Christ.

In my decades of evangelism, it was the first time anyone had told me that they didn't know who Jesus was, and they had never even heard His name. As I dialogued with the men, the familiarity of the situation reminded me of Acts 17. In Paul's many travels to foreign lands, his message of Jesus Christ was completely new to the locals. He was working with a clean slate, so to speak.

In that moment, I felt the same way. There was no need for apologetics. Only an introduction; a declaration of who Jesus was and *is*.

I took that opportunity to give them a copy of *May I Ask You a Question?* and explained the gospel to them. I was confident they were prepared for the contents of that booklet, and they assured me that they would read it.

Imagine, in the twenty-first century, the name of Jesus is still reaching the ears of "those who have not heard."

The Real Hero of the Story

While in Winterset, Iowa, during a speaking trip, I was making calls to our financial contributors to thank them for their support. One woman I've known for years had a genuine concern for the lost. She told me of a friend who attended a very liberal church, and she shared a conversation this lady had with her pastor.

"Do you think if I watch a John Wayne movie," she asked him in complete seriousness, "God will let me into heaven?"

Apparently, this gal thought that John Wayne was a good friend of Jesus Christ. Perhaps, if she watched his movie, she would find "favor by association" and increase her chances of getting into heaven. The pastor's answer makes little difference. God knows the true intent of each and every heart and where we stand with Him. However, it did give my friend the opportunity to share her own testimony with the woman, and explain the need for us to trust in Christ alone to enter into our heavenly home.

It's an example of the lengths Satan will go to in order to get us off track—no matter how far-fetched or ridiculous it seems. He doesn't care what you trust in, as long as you're not trusting in Christ.

Being Radical

A few years ago, there was a camper who came to Pine Cove Christian Camp whose name was Seth. Seth was a high school student at the time, and it was obvious to the staff that he was different than most of their campers. He wore a tough exterior, and his words and actions made it clear he wasn't a believer.

Seth arrived on a Sunday, and by Tuesday he was so angry that it was affecting the other campers. The camp director confronted him, and Seth began to lash out verbally, threatening to hurt the people around him. At that moment, the director told him that he was going home, and he called Seth's father asking him to pick up his son immediately.

Before Seth left camp that night, the director decided to put one of EvanTell's *Ignorant Bliss* gospel tracts in Seth's bag, hoping that as the young man reflected on the love shown to him that week, God would use the Bad News/Good News message to turn his life around.

The next night, the director found a phone message sent from Seth, saying how he had trusted Christ and became a believer the day after he was sent home from camp. When the director returned Seth's call, he asked the once angry youth what had happened.

"When I got home, I looked in my bag and saw a pamphlet. I read through it and believed the truths laid out in it."

Later that summer, Seth returned to camp, radically changed.

I Have an Announcement!

Each year, I have the privilege of leading a number of students to Christ who are just graduating high school. Many of them have never completely understood the plan of salvation. On one such trip, a male student I spoke with was extremely emotional.

His mother had committed suicide when he was only fourteen years old, which created a number of problems for him, none more tragic than his bitterness toward God. The inner pain and anxiety he struggled with was apparent as he openly wept in front of me. Then he listened as I gently shared the truth about God's grace and its ability to heal his broken heart. He then realized what he had to do: trust Christ, and permit God to put his shattered life back together again.

Standing there, he allowed himself to trust Christ. Words cannot describe what happened next. A peace and tranquility came over him, and a smile so big that his face could hardly contain it. I encouraged him to tell two people what had happened, and to do it before the night was out.

I discovered later that after I had left, he went to the microphone and announced to the students that he trusted Jesus.

Sometimes, all we need is a gentle dose of grace.

Stories from the Field

A Letter from Pamela

In an age of email, Twitter, and social media that separates us from connecting on a human level, I treasure letters of the past that touch my heart and emotionally feed my spirit. The following is a letter that needs no explanation:

Dear Dr. Moyer,

> *I just wanted to personally thank you for the deep impact your ministry has made in my life. I am currently attending Dallas Theological Seminary as a Biblical Counseling student.*
>
> *Several years ago, before I knew the Lord, I was attending Word of Life Bible Institute. Your evangelism class changed my life—ultimately, God changed my life—but the way you faithfully presented the gospel led me to not only put my faith and trust in my Lord but was also used by God to call me to ministry.*
>
> *I was in a dark place when I first came to WOLBI, and God had already been working on softening my heart several months before you arrived that fall. During your week of teaching, through the gospel I first realized what grace really was. I saw the attitude of my heart and my life decisions were so incredibly broken. But through that brokenness, God was finally able to bring me to a place of redemption and healing. Not only did God use you to show me how to communicate*

God's truth more effectively and clearly, but God used your faithful service to bring a broken woman before the throne of grace and show me Jesus.

As you were teaching Bible school students how to share the gospel, the gospel was presented to my heart, and I chose to trust Christ. All in all, I just wanted to say thank you. Thank you for the impact you had in my life. Thank you for the amazing way God used you unknowingly as part of God's beautiful master plan for me. The precious gospel which completely and radically changed my life is now the very same gospel that I am so unbelievably passionate about sharing with others.

Thank you for your kind and faithful service, Dr. Moyer!

Blessings,
Pamela

It Never Gets Old

Traveling to a church in southern California, I was there for one of our *You Can Share a Sunday* weekends. It consisted of a message given to excite people about evangelism and then a seminar to train them.

In between the service and the seminar, everyone mingled at a potluck lunch. An orthopedic surgeon sat down next to me and began to explain that he was searching to discover what Christianity was all about. Listening, I could tell that he was confusing the

Christian way of life—living it—with the free gift of grace found in the Giver of that life—Jesus Christ.

The surgeon stayed for the seminar, and afterwards we met again to continue our conversation. He took in all that I had said regarding the plan of salvation as I used the *May I Ask You a Question?* booklet. Then he shared that he at last understood the gospel. In those moments, he trusted Christ to save him.

I gave him the assurance of salvation from John 5:24 and, upon returning to the office, sent him EvanTell's *31 Days to Living as a New Believer*. It never gets old—the exhilaration I feel when explaining the gospel to unbelievers as they come to understand it for the very first time.

Sowing a Future Harvest

In 2012, during an outreach trip to Buckeye, Arizona, I had just finished eating lunch with the pastor when a man came up to me as we were leaving the restaurant.

"You're Larry Moyer, aren't you?"

"Yes, I am," I replied, curious to know how he recognized me. He went on to share a story.

"Back in 1988, you came to speak in Del Rio, Texas. My background was Mormon. I was having trouble figuring out if there was something wrong about that, and what the truth was about grace."

The man was so deliberate as he told his story, it gave me a sense that the information told of a pivotal moment in his life. He continued, "You were one of three people

God used to enable me to understand grace and come to the point where I could trust Jesus Christ as my personal Savior. I'm not sure exactly when I crossed that line, but I do know you were one of three people God used to get me there. I can't tell you how excited I am to see you. I never thought I'd have this chance."

I thanked him for sharing his testimony with me and prayed he would continue to serve God in the lives of those around him. As we parted, I was encouraged to see the fruit of our ministry twenty-four years later.

We plant seeds, we water them, then we move on. We don't always have the opportunity to witness the fruit of that labor. But it's times like these that reinforce the need to keep sowing and watering, knowing that there is a bountiful harvest being produced, whether we see it in this life or in the one to come.

Fifteen

The Plane Truth

> *Now then, we are ambassadors for Christ, as though God were pleading through us: we implore you on Christ's behalf, be reconciled to God.*
> 2 Corinthians 5:20

I feel like I've spent half of my life on airplanes, and I'm certain it's by divine appointment. God seems to have an affinity for a captive audience. Many times, He sequestered someone in order to get their full attention: Moses in the desert; John on Patmos; Paul imprisoned. And those were devoted men of God. But what about folks who have never understood the power of the cross, or what Christ's sacrifice means regarding their eternal security?

Equipped with the booklet *May I Ask You a Question?* (MIAYQ) with its Bad News/Good News presentation, I've engaged more people in lively exchanges than this one chapter can accommodate. I've found that asking provocative questions can open the door to much needed dialogue:

What do you think the future holds for most of us?

Why does it seem that problems in the world are getting worse, not better?

Do you enjoy reading about religious topics?

You hear a lot of people talk about Christ and Christianity; who do you think Christ was?

You may discover that these simple yet probing queries can bring a variety of responses and revelations that can be difficult for some to acknowledge while easy for others to embrace. Though you may not always find a warm reception, the important thing is to engage!

What a pleasure it's been to rub elbows (literally) with people who have yet to find their way to the Truth. The following conversations concerning heaven and the way to get there are based on biblical knowledge found in Romans 3:23, 6:23, 5:8, and Ephesians 2:8-9. I encourage you to read these passages to prepare yourself for personal interaction with others when the Lord arranges those opportunities.

A Few Precious Words

During my return to Dallas from a hunting excursion in Arizona, my connection at the Phoenix airport included a conversation with a woman who appeared distraught. I asked her where she was flying to and she said Chicago—something about it being a sudden and unwanted trip. I asked her what she meant.

"My son was just killed."

"I'm so sorry to hear that. Was it a car accident?"

Her eyes grew moist as she whispered to me the entire truth, "He committed suicide. His wife found him. We thought he was doing fine, but obviously he wasn't."

As we were approaching the ticket counter, there wasn't sufficient time to talk further, but God knows these things in advance. I took a MIAYQ pamphlet from my pocket and wrote on the back, "I am praying for you," and gave it to her before we were separated.

After reading my note, her gaze fastened to me, clearly moved by my sympathy and concern. Though there was so much more to be said, the Lord gives grace where grace is needed. I was just grateful to have been there in those valuable moments when she needed to hear a few precious words of support.

To be available and to bless is to be like Christ.

Let Me Think About It

On a flight from Dallas to Tanzania via a London connection, the gentleman sitting next to me was on his way home to Spain. At first, he kept his headphones on but eventually put them aside.

"What takes you to Tanzania?" he asked.

"I'm in ministry—I'm a speaker."

As I shared a few details about the trip, I made a point of telling him that I didn't believe a person's church affiliation was as important as knowing for certain that they are destined for heaven.

Planes around the world have provided great opportunities for the gospel

When I introduced the MIAYQ booklet, he was intrigued and continued to ask questions as we reviewed it. Like many people I interact with, the man was surprised to hear that eternal life was a free gift.

"But how do you go about receiving this free gift?" he asked.

"It comes by simply trusting Christ. You can express to God what you're doing—in prayer, if you like. We could pray right now if it's something you're comfortable with."

"I think I just need more time to think about this. It's different from what I've been told."

His demeanor was genuine, and I encouraged him not to delay, as no one is promised tomorrow. Also, that he could trust Christ wherever he was—in the privacy of his bedroom, backyard, office, anywhere. With that, I gave him the booklet, which he took appreciatively. In the end, it was *his* decision, as it is for everyone.

This scenario rings of Matthew 13 and the parable of the sower. The soil we sow in varies. Some seed we sow falls by the wayside, some on stony places, and some among thorns. But others fall "on good ground and yielded a crop; some a hundredfold."

Let us faithfully sow seeds everywhere we go.

Endless Love

I was on a flight to Hazelton, Pennsylvania, for an Operation Friendship dinner when I struck up a conversation with a man who noticed the book I was reading dealt with spirituality.

"Are you a preacher?" he asked.

"Yes, I am."

He began to share personal difficulties he was having and mentioned how devastated he was that his wife had just left him. With the flight nearly over, we didn't have a chance to speak at great length. But when I discovered he lived in Dallas, I said that I'd love to get together and talk.

"I'd love to," he replied.

He seemed shocked that I would offer my time to him so easily and was touched by the sentiment as we swapped phone numbers. I placed a MIAYQ booklet in his hand and said goodbye.

The day after I flew back into town, I gave him a call, and we met for breakfast the next morning. For nine years, he had played pro football in the NFL—splitting his career between the Buffalo Bills and the Green Bay Packers. Here was a man who had known great success, wealth, fame, and yet no amount of financial security, physical strength or social prestige could help him now.

Pushing pride aside, he shared the circumstances behind his wife leaving him after seven years of marriage. From his portrait, I gathered that she had problems she hadn't dealt with and that there were things in her past she neglected to tell him about.

After listening for a while, I said to him, "Your marriage may be over, but your life isn't. God still wants to make good things happen for you and use you for His glory."

There at the breakfast table, we prayed together, and he trusted Christ. He couldn't get over the fact that God would place him next to me on the plane so I could explain, in detail, the free gift of grace and salvation. We agreed to meet again to begin a time of one-on-one discipleship.

In this life we will have trouble—Jesus said so. And though we are, at times, cast down, we are not conquered. "We are hard-pressed on every side, yet not crushed" (2 Corinthians 4:8a). Earthly loss is inevitable, but God's love is all around.

A Single Link

I was flying back to Dallas from California when I sat beside a businessman formerly from India but now living in the United States. He asked me what I did and that got us on the subject of faith.

He said, "I'm so confused. In India, we're taught that there are many gods. Then I came to America and was told that there is only one God. How do I know which is right?"

"Everything about Christianity," I told him, "stands or falls on the resurrection. If the resurrection is true, everything that Jesus said matters. But if the resurrection is false, nothing He said matters."

I recommended that he read a book called *Who Moved the Stone?* by Frank Morison. He was a British trial lawyer who decided—in his factual, objective manner—that he would write a book disproving Christianity. When he set out to do just that, he realized his case was weak, and he ended up becoming a believer. And it was the resurrection that convinced him the gospel was true. Mr. Morison did write a book, just not the one he intended.

Quite unexpectedly, the Indian businessman reached into his briefcase. "You mean this one?" he said. In his hand was a copy of *Who Moved the Stone?*

"Where did you get that?" I asked, astonished.

"A few of my fellow businessmen in California are Christians, and we've been talking. They gave it to me and asked me to read it before I returned to California. Do you think I should?" he asked, half-committed.

"I think you *must*," I answered. He agreed.

Filled with awe, I marveled at how the Lord connects us for His purpose. I was one of several people in this gentleman's journey—a single link in a loving chain—used by God to bring him to Christ.

Trusting the Gift Giver

While on a flight to Raleigh, North Carolina, a woman seated next to me said, "I saw you writing in the airport, and I thought how unusual that was. Everybody does everything on computers now. You seldom see someone actually handwriting a letter."

"I think with a pen in my hand," I told her, "but have a secretary who types 120 words a minute. So, I write it, and she types it!"

She asked me what I did for a living, and I explained that I was a speaker in the ministry, which she connected to.

"I took two courses in religion in undergraduate school, and there is *so* much you have to remember."

"A lot of people feel that way. But my whole ministry is dedicated to explaining the major message of the Bible—actually, four things that God wants people to know. They're all found in this little booklet."

I handed her MIAYQ, then presented the four points in the Bad News/Good News tract. One: that we are all sinners. Two: the penalty of sin is death. Three: Christ died for us and rose again. Four: we are saved through trusting Christ alone as our only way to heaven.

As receptive to the message as she was, she still wasn't prepared to trust Christ at that moment. I encouraged her to be thinking about what she had learned as I wrote down my name and office phone number in case she had questions when she returned to Dallas.

Her comment, saying that there was so much to remember about religion, can be boiled down to the four truths I laid out before her. That grace is as simple as receiving a free gift we don't deserve and trusting the Giver who paid for it.

Lost and Found

I once sat beside a young woman in her twenties on a flight to Indiana. She was returning from Florida after meeting a man on the Internet. He invited her to fly there to meet him and begin a relationship. When she arrived, he decided he didn't care for her and sent her home.

She went on to tell me that another man in Pennsylvania had gotten her pregnant, but when he found out about it, he refused to have anything more to do with her. As I listened, there seemed to be a theme repeating itself. And in the throes of her codependent love life, she was also being treated for drug addiction.

Learning that I was a minister, she expressed her disappointment with Jesus. She announced that she couldn't trust Him as her Savior because of how He failed her in the past. There were a number of things she asked Him to do for her, which He neglected to do—such as heal her uncle of terminal cancer who later died.

Within these very private snapshots of frustration and failure, in her mind, she thought Christ had wronged her, but nowhere in her thinking had she wronged Him.

This sad story only reinforces a tragedy—that until people see themselves as lost, they will never accept their need for Christ. By God's grace, I took the opportunity to review the Bad News/Good News tract with her. Only He knows if the message took root.

Regardless of whether someone decides to trust Jesus or not, at least we are still able to do what we've been commissioned to do (Matthew 28:18-20). Show the lost the Way and pray.

Our Final Destination

On a flight from Chicago to Dallas, I had a chance meeting with an elderly gentleman who looked weary and in need of rest. His wife had been in the hospital for over a month with a lung tumor suspected to be malignant. At the same time, his daughter had been in an Atlanta hospital for nearly a year with pancreatic cancer.

When he discovered that I was a minister, he told me that he was from a Baptist church in New York and mentioned he golfed with a pastor almost weekly. However, he wasn't currently involved in any particular church.

"Where are you spiritually—do you know if you're going to heaven?" I asked, concerned by the stressful events he was facing.

"No, I don't know the answer to that," he confessed.

Going through the MIAYQ booklet, I gave him the opportunity to trust Christ right then. He declined, citing that he'd have to make too many changes—like go back to church.

"God isn't asking you to come to church," I assured him, "He is asking you to come to Christ. Attending church doesn't save anyone."

But he couldn't make the leap. I secretly questioned his honesty, believing he might be involved in behavior that he didn't want to discuss, much less give up. And though he was dealing with death on three different fronts—his own mortality (being older), his wife's diagnosis, and his daughter's illness—he still wouldn't trust Christ. All I could do was encourage him to keep reading and seeking the Lord.

Strange how we avoid the fact that, at some point, we must leave the body loaned to us. No one is exempt. But how blessed are those of us who have the peace of knowing our destination after that.

The booklet I've used to lead many to Christ

The Anger Within

While traveling to Ohio on an hour-long flight, I spoke with a man who asked me what I did. When I told him, I couldn't ignore the feeling that he was reaching out for help.

He said he was about to marry a woman who lived in Ohio. His first wife resided in Florida where she had custody of their six-year-old son, though their marriage lasted only one year. It was obvious he was harboring intense hatred for her.

The topic of his father was also laden with anger and bitterness. His dad had left him when he was only two weeks old, and he never saw him again—that was thirty years ago. And though in his heart, he wanted to see his dad, he didn't trust himself to be in his company until he had dealt with his hostility toward him, afraid of what he might do.

The mention of his upcoming wedding led me to ask about his religious background. Brought up as a Baptist, he found that the Catholic church was more appealing since his fiancée was Catholic. However, he confessed that he didn't know for sure if he was going to heaven. That enabled me to share the Bad News/Good News with him.

I explained that we are saved through Christ alone; that on the cross, Christ didn't make a down payment for our sins but made the payment in full.

"I'll make sure to read this," he said, before tucking it into this pocket.

When I returned to Dallas, I followed up with a letter but didn't get a response. There is a reason why the Bible tells us, "Do not let the sun go down on your wrath" (Ephesians 4:26b), and I pray that this man will find peace in this new season of life—the Prince of Peace, Jesus Christ.

God or Liar?

From New York to Dallas, I once sat next to a Plano resident who had a friend attending Southwestern Seminary in Fort Worth. However, this particular man was committed to the Muslim faith, believing Christ to be a great prophet but not the Son of God.

When I showed him New Testament passages where Jesus himself affirmed that God was His Father, which in essence made Jesus God also—like Father, like Son—the man reacted as if he had never seen the verses before. I then posed a truth that few Muslims care to wrestle with.

"You realize that if Jesus said He was God but wasn't, then He couldn't be a great prophet because that statement would make Him a liar and a blasphemer."

After contemplating for a minute, the man had no answer. I pressed him a couple of times as a catalyst for conversation, to no avail. He couldn't respond because it's impossible to make Jesus a prophet *and* a fraud.

Hopefully, the Lord will use that truth to spark a debate within the man, which will eventually lead him to Christ. I left the MIAYQ tract in his hands and prayed silently that God would reveal Jesus to him in all of His divine sovereignty.

Small World, Big God

Sometime in the early 1980's, I was flying to a speaking engagement—where I can't recall. I only remember being pleasantly surprised when the woman sitting next to me turned our conversation to spirituality, asking me about my salvation. She was the first and *only* person in my years of travel to bring up the topic to me before I had a chance to breach the subject with her.

Just returning from a retreat, she said the Lord had convicted her about the need to be bolder in talking about her faith and, therefore, was acting on her commitment to be more evangelistic.

In the fall of 2011, thoughts of our chat came to mind just as they had many times before. I said to the Lord in prayer one morning, "I sure would love to see her again. I wonder whatever became of her."

In the Spring of 2012—some thirty years after meeting her—I was speaking in Baton Rouge. After the morning service, a woman approached me and said, "Dr. Moyer, I'm sure you don't remember me, but I'm Kim. We sat next to each other on a flight."

Thrilled with the way God had answered my prayer, I was filled with awe at His kindness to bring us back together again. Kim continues to walk with the Lord, exercising a boldness that she sought, even training to refine her skills at our *How to Talk to Your Relatives about Spiritual Things* seminar.

The world is a small place when in the company of a big God.

Open Minded People

While on my way back to Dallas from teaching at the Word of Life Bible Institute in New York, next to me sat a professor from the University at Albany. His Jewish background did little to defer him from discussing Christianity, much to his credit. He wasn't at all intimidated by new ideas or differing opinions.

His broad knowledge of religious subject matters—the difference between Calvinism and Arminianism, teachings within the gospels, the letters of Paul the apostle, etc.—enticed him to visit Jerusalem on several occasions, which only stoked his love of studying and absorbing biblical information.

To that end, he asked me the typical questions I've come to expect from non-Christians: "How could a loving God send anyone to hell? What about people who have never heard of Christ, and why would they be lost from God forever? Why is it that goodness won't get a person to heaven?"

Though he had no personal point of reference regarding the gospel of grace, he cordially opened that door for me to present the theology to him. In addition to leaving him with a copy of MIAYQ, I offered three book titles for him to read and discuss with me later: *Who Moved the Stone?* by Frank Morison; *Evidence That Demands a Verdict* by Josh McDowell; and *The Case for Christ* by Lee Strobel.

"Which one would you suggest I start with?" he asked.

I recommended *Evidence That Demands a Verdict*.

"Then I'll do it," he promised.

A few weeks later, I followed up with a letter that mentioned the book *Betrayed* by Stan Telchin.

My encounter with him illustrates why it's so important not to typecast or label folks. Because he was Jewish, some might believe him unwilling to discuss Christ and the possibility that He was the Messiah. This gentleman definitely did not believe Jesus was the Son of God, but at the same time, he wasn't at all offended by the idea, just as I wasn't defensive about his opinions.

Only the Lord knows what happened after that open dialogue between us. The truth is, friendly dialogue is a good thing. I wish more Christians would hone their skills in listening and loving those with opposing views.

Everyone Needs a Hero

As I was flying to Los Angeles for a speaking engagement, the Brazilian businessman next to me was headed to California for his job. His English was fluent, and he could read it even better. I asked him where he was from, and then shared that I was a minister and had visited Brazil the previous year lecturing at the Word of Life Bible Institute.

"I read the Bible every day, although there are parts I don't understand," he admitted. "But Jesus Christ is my hero."

The phrase was like music. These days, the word "hero" is tossed around liberally, and its meaning has been

The Plane Truth

diluted to a weak facsimile of its true stature. What an awesome way to talk about the One who truly deserves our respect and adoration.

"You said that Jesus Christ is your hero. What He really wants to be is your Savior," I said, as I watched for his reaction. "Would you like me to show you in the Bible how you can be certain that you are going to heaven?"

"Yes, I would," he quickly answered.

We spent the next half hour going through the Bad News/Good News tract, and he was simply astonished by the free gift of eternal life and that we are saved by trusting Christ alone.

"If you like, we could pray right now and tell God that you're trusting His son."

"I would like that very much," he said.

We closed our eyes and prayed together aloud. Then, as I often do, I asked the two questions that, for me, seal the deal:

"So, if you were to die right now, where would you go?"

"To heaven," he replied, as confident as could be.

"If you stood before God and He asked, 'Why should I let you into heaven?' what would you tell Him?"

"That I've trusted Jesus Christ as my only way to heaven."

There wasn't a doubt in my mind that he knew exactly what that meant, and we went on to talk for quite some time. He was so amazed by what had happened, he asked if he could keep the tract, and if I could spare a few more for some of his coworkers who were also on the flight.

The last thing he said to me before deplaning was, "I can't wait to go home and share this with my wife. I don't believe she's *ever* heard this before."

When I think about a true hero, it's someone who gives selflessly to others, sacrificing their own safety to save those in a desperate situation. What a perfect way to describe Jesus—His life, death, and resurrection. That's a true Hero!

Sixteen
Big Game, Bigger Reward

> *For since the creation of the world His invisible attributes are clearly seen, being understood by the things that are made, even His eternal power and Godhead, so that they are without excuse.*
> *Romans 1:20*

Where the emerald green isles of western Canada meet the deep navy blue of the Pacific Ocean, my commercial flight descended into Vancouver, British Columbia. There I was met by my hunting guide and boarded a small float plane. Over furrowed wilderness, we dropped into a sparkling patch of azure-colored water tucked between forested crests called Colt Lake and landed.

My first five attempts at hunting mountain goat yielded little more than a number of demanding climbs and long days sitting without a whisper of the illusive creature. With 90% of the world's mountain goats found in this particular area—at heights reaching 3,000 to 13,000 feet—my fortune seemed to hinge on the next trip, always the next trip. This was my sixth attempt at pursuing that highly prized trophy. All other endeavors were fruitless due to not finding the appropriate goat—either it was a nanny with her kids (which is illegal), not locating the size I wanted, or not seeing a goat at all.

Mountain hunting is not for the faint of heart, and if there was a ridge that came with a warning for those less physically capable, it never deterred me. A steep ascent that daunted other hunters only fueled my resolve to conquer it.

We left the lodge on horseback for the base of the mountain, then continued on foot up the sharp incline in search of our elusive quarry. Because mountain goats live at a higher altitude than any other big game, hiking that tests both endurance and tenacity is built into the hunt. It's there, at the very top, that mountain goats watch for dangers below.

The range we undertook on this trip was made of three interconnected mountains, the third being the tallest where we had the best chance of finding success. Reaching the summit, we kept vigil combing the terrain for a target. We spotted one a half-mile away and decided to go after him due to his respectable size.

As I navigated closer, I managed to position myself at a higher elevation where I could look down at him. While he kept a watchful eye for intruders below, I tracked him from a mere 30 yards above. The only thing he saw when he turned was my 7mm rifle just as I pulled the trigger. The bullet entered just behind the shoulder, sparing the animal from prolonged suffering.

Big Game, Bigger Reward

My mountain goat – a majestic creature

He collapsed on a level plain, saving a violent tumble down the mountainside. The guide and I skinned him onsite, taking the meat with us, but leaving the carcass for the varmints who now surely caught the scent of a kill clinging to the breeze. And so ended my first and only mountain goat score—a thrilling achievement.

Bear This in Mind

Sikanni River Valley is nestled in the Canadian Rockies about 120 miles north of St. John in beautiful British Columbia. We flew in via a single engine two-seater and touched down on a narrow strip of land surrounded by forest. My hunting guide lived in the valley and knew where to find one of the biggest, most dangerous omnivores in northern America—the mighty grizzly bear.

This zenith of the forest food chain preys on everything. Nothing preys on it.

My guide and I watched for three days in an area where we found fresh scat, tracks, and claw marks burrowed into trees, marking his territory. A male grizzly can weigh up to eight hundred pounds, and a female's weight can reach six hundred pounds, both eating nearly ninety pounds of roots, berries, and meat a day. Known for their explosive power, a grizzly bear can bring down an adult moose with one swipe of its formidable paw.

It's well known that a bear—be it black bear, polar bear, or grizzly—will proactively attack for two reasons: to protect family and defend food. A sow will aggressively guard her cubs, even against a bear twice her size. This is an animal that requires a human's utmost respect.

Hidden within our hunting blind at the base of a tree, we waited through the days, and returned to the lodge each night, without a sighting. Then, without fanfare or ceremony, a massive grizzly lumbered out into the clearing. My guide spied him first.

"Here he comes," he said, intently.

Lifting my rifle, I stared through the scope, pointing the barrel at his imposing shoulder blade. He was a five-hundred-pound "silvertip," his heavy coat shimming with a metallic sheen down the center of his broad back. His face was resplendent and strong.

I pulled the trigger and my heart pounded as he jumped forward and darted down a ravine. Keep in mind, this was the most dangerous moment of a hunt—not knowing if it was a good shot or a bad one. A good shot would kill the game immediately. A bad shot would only wound the animal, leaving it in pain and aggressive.

The grizzly – an animal to be feared

As we made our way up the ravine—guns at the ready—we found him, lifeless. It was a perfect shot. I had wanted a grizzly for forty years, and I finally had him, on my first grizzly bear hunt. With this trophy accomplished, I could finally put that dream to rest. A score of this magnitude would satisfy me for a lifetime.

The Pride of Boone and Crockett

Not in the rugged outback of the Rockies, but in the lower farmland of Saskatchewan, my close friend, Ray Jones, and I set out for whitetail deer. Autumn in Canada can be unforgiving, and we were prepared for weather twenty degrees below zero. But the temperature was unusually warm that week in November—just below freezing—and we were spared.

When pursuing game that lives at lower elevations, such as deer, a hunting buddy isn't necessary. And with the memory of Ray lost on a sleet-soaked mountainside all night stored safely in the past, this trip required less caution, yet provided plenty of excitement.

We arrived on a Monday and planned to stay through Sunday. Each morning before daylight drifted onto the horizon, our guide would escort us from the lodge to our separate blinds, then return later in the afternoon to check on us. Unlike Ray who took his deer earlier in the week, I would tarry from sunup to sundown until day five before the tide turned in my favor.

It was on Friday when a big, beautiful buck (the largest I've seen in the wild), appeared over the ridge about eighty yards from me. Sure-footed, his awesome silhouette wandered through shaded woods as I held my cloaked position at the edge of the tree line.

At first, he didn't notice me as he lifted his majestic hoofs to slowly trod the underbrush and frozen leaves shed earlier that fall. As he moved closer, I raised my rifle, peering through the scope praying for the opportunity to take the shot. Then, he spotted the blind, froze, and gazed straight at me. It wasn't the angle a hunter hopes for—head-on.

To humanely take down an animal, one patiently delays in hopes of aiming for the body as the game is paralleling you. It is preferred to hit the lungs for a quick death. You never want to cause an animal needless misery.

Big Game, Bigger Reward

And for a few breathless moments, we just looked at each other. If he turned to the right or the left, I would lose him in the trees.

If I could have scripted this scene, he would walk toward me along the ridge, broadside—which is exactly what he did. I couldn't believe it. He moved slowly, giving me the cleanest shot I could have ever wanted.

Suddenly, finding my rifle barrel extended through the blind, the buck nervously backed away from me, leaving me with a split-second decision.

I fired, and the sound ricocheted around the mountain as I watched the buck absorb the bullet's impact. Somersaulting backwards, he crawled another fifty yards and exhaled for the last time. It was a relief to know he was dead within thirty seconds. His sturdy, marbled antlers gave him a stately splendor, with six points on one side and seven points on the other. What a glorious creature!

When the guide returned that afternoon, we loaded the buck onto his 4-wheeler ATV and brought it back to the lodge where Ray joined me in celebrating. He was so happy, as he always was, when fate smiled on me.

This whitetail deer scored just over 176 on the Boone and Crockett Club system—an institute founded by Teddy Roosevelt in 1902. Humbled, it placed me in the upper 5% of all hunters. Few folks get a buck over three hundred pounds that scores so high, as I did. If not for the fifty-six years of hunting experience, I couldn't have managed it. The guide said it was one of the largest bucks ever taken in western Canada.

A whitetail of this size is one few hunters see

On a personal note, you should know that Tammy and I live on wild game, and we appreciate and respect the life of each and every animal, great and small.

The Heart of the Matter

In 2020, cardiovascular disease in this country was recorded to have taken a life every thirty-four seconds; that's 697,000 that year alone—one in five deaths.[6] As I've mentioned, my family history has its share of

---

6 https://www.cdc.gov

fatalities with the loss of my grandfather, father, brother, and uncle to heart attack. It's the reason I've always made a point of being physically active, a habit I started right after graduating from seminary.

A twelve-minute cardiac stress test can reveal the inner-stopwatch of a seasoned athlete or a beleaguered drumbeat of a weakened heart muscle losing steam. I felt blessed that my life had dodged the DNA bullet my beloved family members had fallen victim to.

Between 2011 and 2012, I climbed to the top of five Canadian mountains on hunting expeditions—one of those peaks, a total of six times. I've always watched my diet and run three miles a day for 35 years (excluding when my speaking schedule wouldn't allow), bringing the grand tally to no less than 31,000 miles in my lifetime. And out of an abundance of caution, I schedule biannual checkups with my cardiologist, including EKGs and CT scans. None of them have ever raised red flags. I felt very fortunate.

But just because a person does everything right—exercises, eats well, and manages stress—it doesn't guarantee perfect health.

After undergoing the usual treadmill exam at my cardiologist's office, I headed out of Dallas to Illinois on a hunting trip in November of 2012 while I waited for the results. Tammy drove with me. In hindsight, I guess leaving town without telling my physician wasn't the best idea under those circumstances. It's true that a small percentage of people who have a heart condition show no symptoms until it's too late. *But that wasn't me,* I thought.

It was a clear morning as I sat in a deer blind. Like my prey, not suspecting a thing—a deadly thing just out of sight before it strikes. The phone rang.

"Larry, where are you?" It was my doctor.

"I'm in Illinois, deer hunting," I replied, cheerfully. Surely cardiologists have a happy place they retreat to, like the side of a cold mountain, a rain-drenched deer blind, or a sun-doused valley with abundant game.

"When are you coming back?" he continued without a break.

"Sunday afternoon," I said, as it was now Thursday.

"You failed your stress test. Please, don't do anything strenuous and get back here. I need to see you on Monday."

I admit, that was *not* a call I was expecting.

Sunday morning, as Tammy and I drove home, I was tearful when telling her what the doctor said. With my family history, this wasn't something we took lightly. My sweet wife comforted me while wondering why it took so long for me to share the vital information. I explained that I didn't want to ruin the time spent with her dear relative whom we were visiting. As always, she understood.

The test revealed a 90% blockage in the artery known as the left anterior descending (LAD), which supplies blood to the larger, front part of the heart. The failure of this artery is infamously known as a "widowmaker" heart attack. Stealth is its main character trait, leaving its subject unaware of the threat until there is little time to respond. With this major artery blocked, I had been living on God's good grace.

Hiking up and down mountain peaks, trudging through thick forests and valley beds, lugging heavy hunting gear, it all came rushing back. *Lord, how am I still here?*

Believing that a stent would correct the situation, my cardiologist discovered during the procedure that, instead, a double bypass was needed. The next day, a meticulous heart surgeon by the name of Dr. Mark Pool would see me through the operation. I remained in the hospital for three days before going home to recover. It only took a week longer for me to return to the office and another month before I was back on a treadmill doing my usual three miles a day—more grace.

God not only saved my life each time I climbed a mountain, but He has also added many years to my life since then, courtesy of His loving kindness.

Dr. Pool and I would become the best of friends, and he joined EvanTell's Board of Directors. This godly man, who asks permission from his patients to pray before every surgery, revealed that, if he had known who I was, he would have declined to operate for fear of making a mistake and possibly ending the life of a man God was greatly using. I was so touched by that comment and so grateful he did not decline.

A day, a month, a year. How long we're here, it's impossible to know. But deep within me I am sure, as the moon meets the midnight sky, God has our days numbered and our destiny written in His Book of Life. And if we pay attention, we will see that the Lord is gracious to supply our every need.

Wild Game Feast

In 2009, during the Great Recession, the finances of ordinary households were strained. It became a hardship for cash-strapped couples to invite guests to their church's Operation Friendship dinners. With the rising cost of each plate, it was necessary for EvanTell to pivot in order to meet the needs of folks, just as we had done before.

"The message never changes but the method must."

Then I got to thinking, *I have never had a "burden" for Christians the way I do for non-Christians. I love them. I care about them. But I'm an evangelist called to minister to an unbelieving world. I came to Christ through nature, and I'm an avid hunter. I've also had great success acquiring numerous trophies. That could be an amazing way to bring people to Christ—a Wild Game Feast!*

Replacing the Operation Friendship dinners with Wild Game Feasts (WGF) quickly became, and remains, my primary outreach and passion project.

Similar to Operation Friendship, the local church hosts the gathering but, instead of in a restaurant, it is held in their worship facility or gymnasium. In place of a spiritually-based program, it is a collection of like minds sharing their love of all things outdoors—nature, wild animals, hunting, fishing, hiking, camping, boating, kayaking, etc. And from an evangelistic standpoint, it has been far more effective at getting out the gospel message than any other event we've offered.

Everyone is welcome. From teens to seniors, all ages are coming to Christ through the WGF. Christian men are accompanied by their nonbelieving wives, and Christian women bring their nonbelieving husbands. A common response among church pastors is that they've never had an event where so many nonbelievers are in attendance.

Since 2009 to 2022, there have been nearly 100 WGF gatherings, averaging 54% nonbeliever attendants. At times, it's difficult for the church to find a large enough venue to accommodate everyone interested in going.

Every house of God should have this problem.

The church is encouraged to ask for a $10 donation. It's based on the concept that things of value should cost *something*. To attend a "free" affair might, to some, diminish its worth. In the case of a WGF, participants are more than happy to pay the fee.

A Wild Game Feast is a full evening of fun and festivities. The atmosphere resonates outdoor life with wild game mounts and slideshows of personal community photos, bringing local outdoors people together in solidarity. The colorful table centerpieces are often adorned with luxurious pheasant feathers, antlers, and richly finished wooden candleholders. Doors open at 5:00, dinner at 6:00, my presentation at 7:00, and door prizes—upwards of 50 to 100 gifts donated by local merchants—are given out from 8:00 to 9:00 p.m.

During my talk, I share over one hundred personal hunting photos while telling the stories behind them—some harrowing, others hilarious. This includes hunting trips where I gained a trophy which can inspire guests to go out and do the same. At the end of the presentation, I share my testimony.

As for the menu, some folks bring their own wild game to eat: elk, deer, pheasant, dove, quail, duck, turkey, squirrel, alligator, rabbit, rattlesnake, frog legs, goat, and foreign field game. Others enjoy more traditional meat also served, such as beef, pork, or chicken.

The guests revel in the company of fellow outdoors people (their tribe) and, together, are highly receptive to the gospel. It's gratifying to see this all-inclusive ministry at work, with 10% to 15% of attendees being women. One woman from a local fishing store who donated twelve fishing rods for door prizes, asked the pastor, "Will you let me do this again next year?" The spirit of comradery is a plentiful mix of generosity and zeal. There are folks who have no interest in spiritual things yet, simply by listening and learning about Christ in a relaxed and welcoming setting, are coming to Jesus.

Firsthand accounts and testimonies from attendees alone could fill a book. Like the teenager who moved in with his grandfather to escape his dad's violent anger and came to Christ at the WGF. The next morning, he returned for the Sunday service and brought his sister who also trusted the Lord. There was a man who had "no time for God" but came to Christ through WGF and is now being discipled. And yet another teenager in Nebraska interested in the outdoors, but not in spiritual matters, ended up a believer and has since gone on to serve on international mission trips sharing the gospel.

I feel that enjoying the outdoors of this earth is only a faint precursor to taking in the extravagant sites found in the kingdom of heaven. "For now we see in a mirror, dimly, but then face to face. Now I know in part, but then I shall know just as I also am known" (1 Corinthians 13:12). How privileged we are to have been given such a dwelling, brimming with wonder.

Wild Game Feasts – a tremendous outreach

To be a steward of God's spectacular beauty is no small appointment. Wilderness, oceans, rivers, mountains, and valleys . . . *and people*. They are all on loan, placed in our care. And with all of the traveling I've done—across this country and worldwide—hunting, speaking, and teaching, nowhere do I feel more useful than in the same place I've always found it.

In the center of God's will.

Seventeen

The Mission Continues

*And the things that you have heard from me among
many witnesses, commit these to faithful men
who will be able to teach others also.*
2 Timothy 2:2

Since before the conception of EvanTell to present day, God has spoken to me through prayer, meditation, and study. He has reached out, despite my shortcomings, to raise up a ministry dedicated to shining a light on the gospel message, bright enough for the world to see and hear the truth about Christ. This miracle of God is not surprising. But what is astonishing is that, in His infinite power and goodness, He has graciously used *me*—of all people—to speak for Him.

What a gift it is to be used by the One called Jesus!

Over the decades, a few rebellious gray hairs have multiplied into many as less of their youthful cohorts stake their claim. A stronger prescription for eyeglasses holds no shame, and an occasional twinge from protesting bones make their case. The lines on my face foretell of a time when my work here will be done. When that day comes, I have prayed that this ministry would not only survive but thrive after my last breath is gone.

While some folks may deny the Way to heaven, it only feeds the need within me to spread the good news to those who have yet to hear it.

In the early 1970s, with the birth of a small nonprofit, God convicted me that He wanted this ministry to outlast me—an idea that excited me and one I have honored from the very start. I've always said, "Fifty years from now, you don't have to know who *I was*. You just have to know who *Jesus is*." EvanTell's longevity has always been in the back of my mind, with a fervent plea on my lips: "God, work so mightily through EvanTell that it defies any human explanation so that You alone receive the glory."

And as the calendar kept count of my days, months, and years, I pursued every avenue the Lord opened to me—traveling countless miles, near and far, sharing God's message of grace, planting seeds to the best of my ability.

My dream of a ministry that would still be here after I had gone is the very reason why I chose not to use my name in the association title. The last thing I wanted was to create an organization that fell victim to "Founder's Syndrome"—a dependency on the single person whose identity keeps the ship afloat.

Our former Chairman of the Board, Vaughn Pearson, once said to me regarding leadership, "You don't have to know everything, just surround yourself with the people who do." I decided then to hire people better than myself. Without the entanglements of pride or ego, one is free to embrace those who have gifts he, himself, might personally be lacking, without intimidation or threat.

Suddenly, it was time to actively plan for that fruitful future I had so often thought about. In 2003, we restructured EvanTell, placing several key officers on an executive staff. Those positions included a Chief Operations Officer and a Chief Ministry Officer who would oversee six departments. Eventually those six became four: academics, church, workplace, and community—all with an international focus.

The efforts of this executive staff played an important role in the expansion of EvanTell, impacting millions of people each year. The following fall, with the unanimous support of the Board of Directors, EvanTell charted a way ahead to flourish as a global ministry beyond my lifetime.

In 2007, the board would further delegate the ever-growing ministry responsibilities, adding an Executive Committee, Development Committee, Finance Committee, Human Resource Committee, and Governance Committee. Each team could then bring major items before the board for approval, thus balancing the workload for better efficiency. To their credit, everyone involved in the recalibration of EvanTell did an incredible job and has my sincerest thanks.

Letting Go and Letting God

A mission statement is an important part of any ministry and, in the case of EvanTell, it was my personal promise to God: *EvanTell exists to encourage and equip individuals and churches to reach the world with the clear and simple good news of Jesus Christ.*

As the Founder, CEO, and President, I've had the great joy of watching a fledgling nonprofit blossom, by God's grace, becoming a worldwide evangelistic powerhouse. In 2006, David Souther joined the team to further grow the international ministry. His fingerprints are found on a plethora of projects as he worked diligently on ministry resources and materials. He has taught those materials and placed them into international translations, orchestrating sales into overseas markets, certifying domestic instructors, and speaking on foreign fields.

As the Director of International Ministry, David was instrumental in lightening my load that I might focus my energy in other areas.

Paul Pham was hired in 2008 as Chief Financial Offer. After a decade of dedicated service to our global mission, Paul was diagnosed with liver cancer and lingered for more than a year until his death in May of 2018. The team dealt with a profound sadness at the loss. Since launching EvanTell, Paul was the first person to die while on staff. It was an incredibly hard time for everyone due to our love for him. He was survived by his wife, Sharon, and their three children. Though we soon hired another CFO, Paul's absence touched us deeply, and his memory will never fade.

In 2011, the ministry separated the roles of President and CEO, with the Board of Directors unanimously selecting Andy Coticchio to take the reins of President. Having first joined EvanTell as a board member, Andy had everyone's complete confidence in his abilities. I continued full-time as Founder and CEO, but without the day-to-day duties of running the ministry. This permitted me to center my attention where I was most needed.

It's a beautiful thing to be a part of one body with an abundance of moving parts—all talented and accomplished in a variety of ways. I feel certain that is why Jesus emphasized the need for us to join together in unity. It's difficult to exalt yourself with so many hands and feet doing the work.

It can be tough to let go of things we have done for years. But in 2015 I felt a strange sense of freedom as I turned over increased ministry operations to David Souther. He was now the new President of EvanTell, after Andy had done a great job mentoring him to step into the position when the time came. This change was exactly what I needed to focus solely on evangelism in very specific ways.

Encouraging supporters and ministry staff with a vision of service that furthers the gospel has always been my number one goal, add to that authoring books, articles, and blogs. The written word is a powerful thing, and I've found it to be a great tool to reach people. Where a single person can only be in one place at a time, an article can be in thousands of places at once.

Another aspect of my evangelistic duties is to oversee the Board of Directors, close kin to inspiring and directing special human skills, strategies, and resources. Fundraising is also a much-needed part of enabling a ministry, and phone calls, personal correspondence, emails, in-person contact are all necessary for the health and endurance of EvanTell.

David Souther assumes the main responsibility for EvanTell

Finally, traveling and speaking—both domestically and internationally—is such an enjoyable part of my job as an evangelist. The warmth of humanity enriches all life, and those who receive the gospel's nourishing message benefit as I benefit in sharing it with them.

We all have our individual wants and desires, in ministry and in life, whether designated by God or self-assigned, to feel noticed and loved. Perhaps this is a good reminder that "If we live in the Spirit, let us also walk in the Spirit" (Galatians 5:25). In this way, we can find our true fulfillment as we exercise the unique gifts we've been given.

A New Normal

In 2020, the highly contagious and deadly COVID-19 virus broke out around the world. It's safe to say that it affected the vast majority of people on the planet in some way or another. And like so many other organizations, EvanTell would have to adapt to the changing times.

The pandemic restricted our ability to travel, both in the U.S. and abroad. During this time, I worked closely with our training folks using social media and writing books—adding to the increasing number, now reaching fourteen titles (all found on EvanTell's website at www.evantell.org).

Though the ways we minister to people have evolved, our vision has remained unchanged. My personal hunger for every church to find excitement and enthusiasm regarding evangelism is as prominent now as it was my first day at Dallas Seminary.

Though the world and our surroundings continue to advance in both positive and negative ways, it's my ongoing hope that each house of worship will join me in common prayers that lift up the faithful in the following ways:

To find renewed energy as individuals in their congregations are born again and are thoughtfully discipled.

That every Christian organization is blessed with a spiritually healthy staff and volunteers that are educated, equipped, and empowered to clearly share the gospel.

That indigenous believers in other countries will have the opportunity to be trained in evangelizing their own people, in their own language.

That all Bible colleges and seminaries have excellent evangelistic curriculum to teach future leaders of the church.

That all pastors and lay leaders are well-able to confidently present the gospel messages.

And finally, that each Christian is capable of explaining to their coworkers, friends, strangers, and loved ones how to find eternal life with God through trusting Jesus Christ.

Just as our ministry's vision for the furtherance of the good news has never wavered, neither has its philosophy. EvanTell does not wish to be a large missionary association with individuals supported through their own personal outreach. Instead, it is a home office with numerous EvanTell employees training folks in other organizations, institutions, and churches across the world, reflecting a servant mentality, thus multiplying its impact ten, hundred, and a thousand-fold.

If there is anything I hope those who read this book take away, it is the biblical basis for reaching the lost and training others to do likewise, found in the charge Christ gave to His disciples—and to us!

"Go therefore and make disciples of all the nations, baptizing them in the name of the Father and of the Son and the Holy Spirit, teaching them to observe all things that I have commanded you; and lo, I am with you always, even to the end of the age" (Matthew 28:19-20).

In these verses we have the Great Commission that Christ Himself modeled for us. And though times have changed and will continue to change in the years to come, I can only imagine how much more the gospel will be needed as our world grows steadily darker with the nearing of the Day of the Lord, spoken about in 1 Thessalonians 5:1-11.

As Christians, we have the knowledge that Jesus' return is approaching, and that it will come "as a thief in the night." We have not been left in the darkness, but we are the "sons [and daughters] of light," sober and awake. Let us then wake as many sleeping souls as we can, before the day of reckoning comes.

Let us run the race with perseverance and never lose our love for the Lord and the lost.

I continue evangelizing and training others in evangelism

Conclusion

Through the prophet Isaiah, the Lord tells His people, Israel, "I will strengthen you, yes, I will help you" (Isaiah 41:10b). Thinking back over the years, I too have experienced that strength and help—both carrying me through the greatest challenges and the deepest sorrows of my life. It reminds me of the disciple Paul who, in the midst of every circumstance, surrendered his own will and weakness to Christ, proclaiming, "I can do all things through Christ who strengthens me" (Philippians 4:13).

Through the decades, I have faced disappointment, heartache, and loss. In 2009, when the economy soured, we wondered if our ministry could survive. At times, donations fell far short of expectations, and staff had to be reduced due to budget deficits. Training seminars and outreaches carefully planned were sometimes met with a major hurdle.

But I also felt immense joy and love, guided by the Spirit who makes it possible for a flawed man like me to mend lives and introduce people to Jesus. Not by my own power, but through Christ who makes all things achievable to those who believe. He said that in this world, we would have trouble, but to be cheerful for He has overcome the world. It is a gift and a privilege for us to walk in faith, and that has filled my own journey with miraculous wonders.

As a boy, when my words stumbled, causing humiliation and pain, God was schooling me in empathy. When my calling looked impossible and sadness threatened to leave me in a state of permanent misery, the Lord was preparing me for compassionate service. When I stood at the door of ministry holding nothing but a childhood vision, Christ opened those doors to a lifetime of work that, by all accounts, should never have happened.

But as the tongue of my past made peace with my future, I moved forward in the strength God provided to begin a fifty-year mission that continues to this day. In the oddity that is God's miracles, a nonprofit was born based on presenting the gospel with *clarity* and the careful handling of scripture. My speech impediment was always God's plan to glorify Himself and to spread His message—the same message still boldly spoken through the most unlikely evangelist.

If God can take such a man, and dismiss every negative expectation whispered in his ear and diagnosis documented in a therapist's file, how much more will He use you when you open your heart to His design for your life? What an impact each one of us could make for His kingdom if we all took the path less traveled to reach those lost in a wilderness without Christ.

Now I find myself approaching the sunset of my days and have these few humble things to impart:

Never give up on your calling, no matter who tells you otherwise. Only God "who works in you both to will and to do for His good pleasure" (Philippians 2:13) and

Conclusion

only He can predict your perfect destiny. Believe in *Him*. Rejoice in *Him*. And *He* will bring it to pass.

Be strong in the Lord, and in His strength your divine purpose will be revealed! Know that "In Him we live and move and have our being" (Acts 17:28). With confidence in Christ, take courage and trust, that the race you run now, you will finish well as you submit to His loving embrace.

Finally, if there is a single idea that I would have you remember from this book, the most important point of all, it is to *be clear* when sharing the message of God's good news. So that all who hear it will understand and trust in Christ alone to save them.

Heaven is not far away, and in that eternal home where rest and reward await us, we will be joined together for eternity with the One who made it possible.

The Unlikely Evangelist

Be strong!

We are not here to play, to dream, to drift;

We have hard work to do, and loads to lift.

Shun not the struggle; face it.

'Tis God's gift.

Be strong!

Say not the days are evil—Who's to blame?

And fold the hands and acquiesce—O shame!

Stand up, speak out, and bravely,

In God's name.

Be strong!

It matters not how deep entrenched the wrong,

How hard the battle goes, the day how long,

Faint not, fight on!

Tomorrow comes the song.

~ Maltbie D. Babcock

Acknowledgments

A heartfelt thanks to my sweet wife, Tammy, for the way God has used her to make my ministry possible. Only eternity will fully reveal the impact she has had upon me personally and upon this ministry.

My son, David, has always supported me. I have felt that support beside me in the car while we ran Saturday morning errands together as well as when we were thousands of miles apart as I ministered overseas.

Dad, one Saturday morning through hunting, started me down a path that ultimately led to the Savior and birthed my story.

To my mentor Dr. Haddon Robinson; you were the one God used to teach me the difference between speaking and communicating, and got me started when nobody knew I was available.

I feel a tremendous indebtedness to Dennis Hillman, who in the mid-nineties encouraged me to expand my ministry through writing, and has been my biggest encourager in that area. This memoir would not have been the same without his input.

Thanks to Joy Kupp for using her God-given ability in editing so much of what I have written over the years, including this book. She is one of the best.

God used the beautiful talent of Kimberly Shumate to cause me to transparently tell my story to her so she would in turn know how to tell it to others.

This book would not have been possible without the administrative skills of my assistant, Shaylana Nelson. It was not only what she did as project manager, but the cheerful and excited attitude in which it was done.

The entire staff of EvanTell has my appreciation for the way they insisted that I tell my story and freed me up time-wise and workload-wise to make it happen.

I will always be indebted to the thousands of church leaders across the world who allowed me to come alongside them as their servant, step into their pulpits, and in so doing, use and develop my gift in evangelism.

Thanks to all of you and many more that time and paper will not allow me to mention for being gifted instruments in the hands of an Almighty God. "I thank my God upon every remembrance of you" (Philippians 1:3).

Appendix

May I Ask You a Question? Tract

EvanTell's "May I Ask You a Question?" tract has been helpful in introducing millions to Christ. The tract can be ordered from EvanTell, Inc., by calling 1-800-947-7359 or by vistiting our online store at www.evantell.org.

Appendix

Has anyone ever shown you from the Bible how you can know for sure you are going to heaven?

The Bible contains both bad news and good news.
The *bad news* is something about YOU.
The *good news* is something about GOD.

Let's look at the bad news first...

Appendix

Bad News 1

We are all sinners.
Romans 3:23 says, *"For all have sinned and fall short of the glory of God."*

"Sinned" means that we have missed the mark. For example, when we lie, hate, lust, cheat, break promises, gossip, etc. we have missed the standard God has set.

May I Ask You a Question? Tract

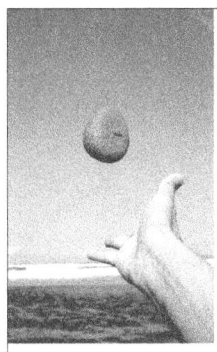

Suppose you and I each threw a rock, trying to hit the North Pole. You might throw farther than I do, but neither of us would hit the goal.

In the same way we all fall short of God's standard of perfection.

In thoughts, words, and actions, we don't even come close to perfect.

But the bad news gets worse...

Appendix

Bad News 2

The penalty for sin is death.
Romans 6:23 says, *"For the wages of sin is death."*

When we are hired to do a job, we get paid. That money is our wages. That is what we have earned.

The Bible says that by sinning we have earned death. That means we deserve to die and be separated from God forever.

But God made a way for us to live and be with Him forever.

APPENDIX

Good News 1

Christ died for you.

Romans 5:8 says, *"But God demonstrates His own love toward us, in that while we were still sinners, Christ died for us."*

Suppose you were in a hospital dying of cancer, and I came to you and said, "Let's take the cancer cells out of your body and put them into my body."

If that were possible,
**What would happen to me?
What would happen to you?**

I would die and you would live.

I would die in your place.

The Bible says Christ took the penalty that we deserved for sin, placed it on Himself, and *died in our place.* Three days later, Christ came back to life to prove that sin and death had been conquered and that His claims to be God were true.

Just as the bad news got worse, the good news gets better!

Appendix

Good News 2

You can be saved through faith in Christ.

Ephesians 2:8-9 says, *"For by grace [undeserved favor] you have been saved [delivered from sin's penalty] through faith, and that not of yourselves; it is the gift of God, not of works, lest anyone should boast."*

Faith means *trust*.

You must depend on Him alone to forgive you and to give you eternal life.

May I Ask You a Question? Tract

Just as you trust a chair to hold you through no effort of your own, *so you must trust Jesus Christ to get you to heaven* through no effort of your own.

But you may say,

"I'm religious."

"I go to church."

"I'm a good person."

"I help the poor."

"I don't do anything that's really bad."

These are all good, but good living, going to church, helping the poor, or any other good thing you might do cannot get you to heaven. You must trust in Jesus Christ alone, and God will give you eternal life as a gift.

Appendix

Is there anything keeping you from trusting Christ right now?

1. _____
2. _____
3. _____
4. _____

Think carefully. Is there really anything more important than your need to trust Christ?

Would you like to tell God you are trusting Jesus Christ as your Savior? If you would, why not pray right now and tell God you are trusting His Son?

It is important to understand that it is not a prayer that saves you. Prayer is simply how you tell God what you are doing.

Dear God, I know I'm a sinner. I know my sin deserves to be punished. I believe Christ died for me and rose from the grave. I trust Jesus Christ alone as my Savior. Thank You for the forgiveness and everlasting life I now have. In Jesus' name, amen.

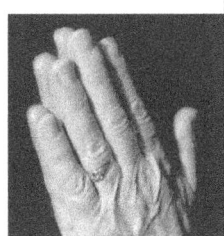

Appendix

What just happened?

John 5:24 explains, "*He who hears My word and believes in Him who sent Me has everlasting life, and shall not come into judgment, but has passed from death into life.*"

» Did you "hear" God's word?
» Did you "believe" what God said and trust Christ as your Savior?
» Does "has everlasting life" mean later or right now?
» Does it say "shall not come into judgment" or might not?
» Does it say "has passed from death" or shall pass?

Eternal life is based on fact, not feeling.

We suggest that you memorize John 5:24 today.

What do you do now?

Having trusted Christ as your only way to heaven, here's how to grow in your relationship with Him.

» Tell God what's on your mind through prayer (Philippians 4:6-7).

» Read the Bible daily, to learn more about Him and learn from Him (2 Timothy 3:16-17). Start in the book of Philippians.

» Worship with God's people in a local church (Hebrews 10:24-25).

» Tell others about Jesus Christ (Matthew 4:19).

APPENDIX

If you have found this booklet helpful, please share it with someone else. If you have further questions about what is contained in this booklet, contact:

The Gospel. Clear and Simple.

PO Box 703929 | Dallas, TX 75370
www.evantell.org | 800.947.7359
© EvanTell, inc.   TRMEN004

GET EQUIPPED & ENCOURAGED
AT EVANTELL.ORG

TAKE OUR FREE PERSONAL EVANGELISM ONLINE COURSES

SEE ALL COURSES AT
EVANTELL.ORG/ONLINE-TRAINING

VIEW OUR TOPIC-BASED TRAINING LIBRARY

BROWSE HOURS OF CONTENT THAT COVER THE HOTTEST TOPICS AT
EVANTELL.ORG/VIRTUAL-EVENTS

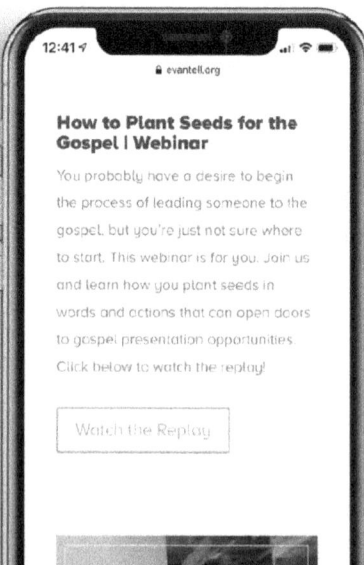

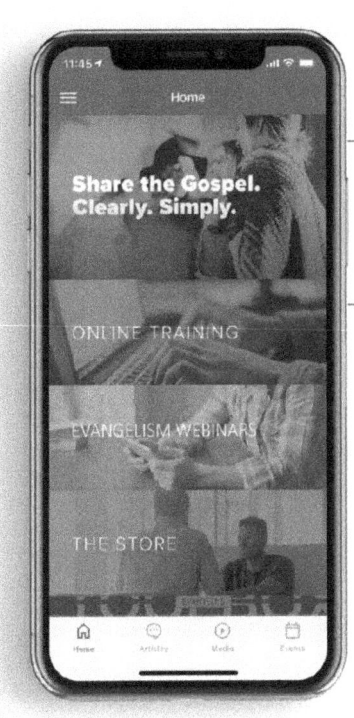

DOWNLOAD OUR APP
FOR EVANGELISM TRAINING
ON-THE-GO

VISIT YOUR APP STORE
AND SEARCH *"EVANTELL"* TO
DOWNLOAD TODAY

VISIT OUR STORE
FOR BOOKS, TRACTS,
AND MORE RESOURCES

VISIT *EVANTELL.ORG/STORE* TO SEE OUR FULL
COLLECTION OF BOOKS AND RESOURCES

www.ingramcontent.com/pod-product-compliance
Lightning Source LLC
Chambersburg PA
CBHW061733070526
44585CB00024B/2653